PERCEPTUAL ORGANIZATION
AND VISUAL RECOGNITION

THE KLUWER INTERNATIONAL SERIES
IN ENGINEERING AND COMPUTER SCIENCE

ROBOTICS: VISION, MANIPULATION AND SENSORS

Consulting Editor

TAKEO KANADE

...UAL ORGANIZATION AND VISUAL RECOGNITION

PER...

by
DAVID G. LOWE
Courant Institute of Mathematical Sciences
New York University

KLUWER ACADEMIC PUBLISHERS
Boston/Dordrecht/Lancaster

Distributors for North America:
Kluwer Academic Publishers
190 Old Derby Street
Hingham, MA 02043, USA

Distributors outside North America:
Kluwer Academic Publishers Group
Distribution Centre
P.O. Box 322
3300 AH Dordrecht
THE NETHERLANDS

Library of Congress Cataloging in Publication Data

Lowe, David G.
  Perceptual organization and visual recognition.

  (The Kluwer international series in engineering and
computer science. Robotics and vision)
  Bibliography: p.
  Includes index.
  1. Computer vision. 2. Visual perception. I. Title. II. Series.
TA1632.L68 1985   001.64'4   85-9762
ISBN 0-89838-172-X

Copyright © 1985 by Kluwer Academic Publishers. Third Printing 2000.

Printed in the United States of America

CONTENTS

v

PREFACE

COMPUTER VISION is a field of research that encompasses many objectives. A primary goal has been to construct visual sensors that can provide general-purpose robots with the same information about their surroundings as we receive from our own visual senses. This book takes an important step towards this goal by describing a working computer vision system named SCERPO. This system can recognize known three-dimensional objects in ordinary black-and-white images taken from unknown viewpoints, even when parts of the object are undetectable or hidden from view. A second major goal of computer vision research is to provide a computational understanding of human vision. The research presented in this book has many implications for our understanding of human vision, particularly in the areas of perceptual organization and knowledge-based recognition. An attempt has been made to relate each computational result to the relevant areas in the psychology of vision. Since the material is meant to be accessible to a wide range of interdisciplinary readers, the book is written in plain language and attempts to explain most concepts from the starting position of the non-specialist.

One of the most important conclusions arising from this research is that visual recognition can commonly be achieved directly from the two-dimensional image without any preliminary reconstruction of depth information or surface orientation from the visual input. This is in contrast to most previous research in computer vision and many theories of human vision which assume that our three-dimensional knowledge of an object's appearance is matched to some kind of corresponding three-dimensional reconstruction from the data in an image. While seemingly solving a more difficult problem—the direct recognition of objects from unknown viewpoints using only two-dimensional data—the approach given in this book is shown to actually be simpler and more reliable. While it is clear that depth-measurement processes such as stereo vision and motion interpretation are important aspects of human vision, it is argued that these are more likely to follow recognition rather than precede it for typical instances of recognition.

How is it possible to recognize an object when we have no idea of the viewpoint from which we will be seeing it? A central role is played by the process known as perceptual organization, in which relations are found directly among the two-dimensional features of an image. The relations that are formed are those—such as collinearity and parallelism—that are present in the image over a wide range of viewpoints. This perceptual organization process corresponds closely to the grouping phenomena of human vision studied by the Gestalt psychologists, but it has been missing from almost all computer vision systems. A second important component of this methodology is a mathematical method for bringing the projection of a three-dimensional model into precise correspondence with the two-dimensional features in an image. This allows the system to exploit the high degree of redundancy in our visual knowledge, since only a few matches are required to determine the viewpoint and we can then make accurate predictions for the locations in the image of all the remaining features of the object. Previous computer vision systems have not made quantitative use of the spatial information in an image to the limits of accuracy of the data. The quantitative method provides a very robust and reliable method for extending and verifying an initial hypothesis. The remaining aspects of matching can be based largely on search techniques borrowed from previous research in artificial intelligence.

The current version of the SCERPO vision system is only a first attempt at combining the various components for which it is named (SCERPO is an acronym for Spatial Correspondence, Evidential Reasoning, and Perceptual Organization). This methodology suggests numerous directions for further research. One of the most exciting topics for further study is in the area of learning, since the probability-based methods of search used in this system make it relatively easy to provide for continuing incremental improvements in performance as the visual system gains experience in its environment.

ACKNOWLEDGEMENTS: This book summarizes research performed over a period of six years, both while I was pursuing my graduate training at Stanford University and recently while I have been at the Courant Institute of Mathematics at New York University. Over the years, many people have made contributions to this research and have provided important help in other ways.

I received a thoughtful and stimulating introduction to computer vision from Alan Mackworth while I was an undergraduate at the University of British Columbia. I then went to Stanford University to pursue my Ph.D. degree. Tom Binford provided the financial support and excellent facilities for performing the research, and made many important contributions to my research. Chapter 5 is based largely on his own work on inferring shape from the image. Andy Witkin helped me to develop the foundations of my approach, and his own work on perceptual organization was a major influence. Brian Wandell contributed many suggestions in addition to helping me over the hurdles of being a graduate student. Rod Brooks was at first a fellow student, but during my last year at Stanford he returned as a professor and was very helpful during the process of completing my thesis. David Marimont was always ready to discuss any topic and offer his excellent ideas. Chris Goad provided help in many ways, and showed me the power of a clear approach to complex problems. I wish him and all the others at Silma Incorporated the greatest of success. Harlyn Baker played a major role in integrating the work in our laboratory and helped my research in many ways. Sid Liebes contributed his extensive knowledge of the details of perspective projection. Some of the others who were particularly helpful include Peter Blicher, John Craig, Mike Genesereth, Benjamin Grosof, Jeff Kerr, Oussama Khatib, Mike Lowry, Allan Miller, Jitendra Malik, Sandy Pentland, Barry Soroka, Marty Tenenbaum, Sandy Wells, and Terry Winograd. While at Stanford, I was partially supported by a four-year National Science and Engineering Research Council of Canada Postgraduate Scholarship. The research also received support under NSF grant DAR78-15914 and ARPA contracts MDA903-80-C-0102 and N00039-82-C-0250.

During the past five months I have been at the Courant Institute of Mathematical Sciences. In spite of the many new responsibilities of being an assistant professor and teaching for the first time, this has also been a productive period for new research. All of the code for the SCERPO vision system was implemented in a period of just three months. Much of the credit for making this such a productive environment must go to the many people who provided important help. Robert Hummel had prepared an extensive programming environment for using the VICOM image processor, which was used to perform many of the preliminary stages of processing required by the system. He has been extremely helpful in both technical and practical ways in all the stages of implementing the SCERPO system. Likewise, Jack Schwartz has provided the full services of the vision and robotics laboratory and many other forms of assistance.

Mike Overton has provided useful advice on the numerical aspects of the implementation. Some of the others who have made this a pleasant working environment include Jim Demmel, Colm O'Dunlaing, Zvi Kedem, Dennis Shasha, Alan Siegel, Olof Widlund, and Chee Yap.

Finally, what would the acknowledgements section of a modern computer science book be without a reference to the layout and typography? This book was typeset using Don Knuth's TeX system and the Computer Modern family of fonts. I would particularly like to thank David Fuchs for his help in obtaining the final output from a high-resolution phototypesetter.

Manhattan, New York   D.G.L.

Chapter 1

INTRODUCTION

THE FIELD of computer vision covers a wide range of topics that are often only loosely related to the capabilities and function of human vision. Computer vision systems may use exotic sensors such as laser rangefinders or make restrictive assumptions regarding the scene that have no counterpart in human vision. However, the following pages will deal mostly with the interpretation of single black-and-white images—in particular with edge descriptions extracted from them—and will not generally make use of restrictive assumptions regarding the scene. This portion of the computer vision problem seems to be one of the most central to the functioning of the human visual system, and much of the following study will be motivated by what is known of human vision.

Our major goal will be to achieve visual recognition. Recognition implies that a correspondence has been found between elements of the image and a prior representation of objects in the world. The importance of this prior world knowledge for solving the problem of vision can hardly be overstated. The objects and scenes that we see in our daily lives, although large in number and variation, constitute only a tiny fraction of the set of theoretically possible visual images. Without the constraining influence of these prior expectations, many visual problems

1

would be underconstrained to the extent that they could never be solved. Recognition enables us to go beyond the data that is in the image, since we can achieve reliable identification from a small subset of the predicted correspondences and then use our knowledge to infer many properties of the scene that may not be directly supported by visual data. This emphasis on world knowledge parallels developments in most other areas of artificial intelligence, in which large amounts of problem-specific knowledge are increasingly being used both to constrain solutions and to speed the process of reaching them. However, this view is not universally accepted within the computer vision community, so we will return to this topic many times in the following pages with demonstrations of the value and necessity of achieving correspondence with world knowledge at the earliest possible level of processing.

Recognition can be achieved through correspondences between many kinds of predicted and measured properties, including shape, color, texture, connectivity, context, motion, or shading. However, most of the content of this book will be focused upon only a single one of these dimensions—the problem of achieving spatial correspondence. By spatial correspondence we mean that the measured locations of features in the image are in accurate agreement with the predicted locations of features for a particular projection of some known object. The features that we will be emphasizing are ones that can be accurately located in the image, such as edge or point discontinuities in intensity. Methods will be presented that operate in this spatial domain all the way from purely bottom-up descriptive processes to final verification of correspondence with a particular object. Why will there be such an emphasis on this single aspect of correspondence? A major reason is that this locational information usually seems to be the strongest source of data in terms of the number of measurements that can be made in a typical image and the accuracy of each measurement in the presence of noise. Furthermore, solving the problem of

spatial correspondence is often prerequisite to examining correspondence along the other dimensions. Region-based properties
such as color, texture or shading are most easily applied only
after spatial correspondences have determined the appropriate
regions to consider. However, we will not ignore these other dimensions entirely, and in Chapter 6 methods will be presented
for using all dimensions of correspondence at an early stage of
processing.

Recognition does not imply that we must know every aspect of an object's appearance prior to recognition. While the
SCERPO vision system described in Chapter 8 makes use of
precisely defined object models—such as might be available to
a robot in an industrial environment—there are many ways to
loosen the specification of the knowledge used by the system.
One method will be described in Chapter 7, in which object
models may be parameterized. In other words, the object may
have variable sizes, angles, or articulations between components,
with expected bounds given for each parameter. These parameters can be solved for simultaneously with solving for viewpoint.
Just as important is the fact that there is no precise boundary between what is an object and what is a component. It is
possible to recognize commonly-occurring components, such as
cylinders, rectangular solids, or repeated patterns, as parameterized objects in their own right. The only requirements are
that there be fewer unknown parameters to the description than
there are useful measurements to be made from the image data,
and that the components occur with sufficient frequency to make
their detection a worthwhile use of computational resources.
These recognized components—even if the identification is only
tentative—can then be used to suggest the identity of the more
specific structure of which they are a part. If the identification
of the components is quite certain, then they can even be combined into previously unknown or very loosely parameterized
relationships. Most objects will be represented both in terms
of their overall shape and in terms of a combination of compo-

nents, and different images can best make use of each type of description depending upon such variables as image resolution, viewpoint, and occlusion.

1.0.1: Viewpoint and spatial correspondence

There is at least one obvious problem in achieving spatial correspondence between a two-dimensional image and prior knowledge of three-dimensional objects: the spatial expectations for the image are highly dependent upon viewpoint. Each viewpoint of a three-dimensional object generally leads to a different spatial projection of features in the image. This has caused many vision researchers to emphasize the need for depth information, or else to discard the spatial information by using region-based properties or patterns of connectivity rather than predicted metric locations. A major topic of this book will be the development of quantitative methods for making use of spatial information in the two-dimensional image. An important component of this is a method to determine whether a set of correspondences are spatially consistent with the projection of an object from a single viewpoint. Chapter 7 presents a method that determines exact viewpoint and values of variable model parameters from a few hypothesized correspondences between model and image. This forms the basis for judging spatial consistency with the model and for enlarging the set of correspondences by making precise locational predictions for further features. The determination of spatial correspondence also makes it easy to determine correspondence between region-based properties. Since the final set of correspondences will typically be greatly overdetermined for most objects, it is possible to make reliable judgements regarding the correctness of an interpretation even in the presence of many missing features or occlusion.

Given that we have a method for reliably determining the correctness of an interpretation, the remaining aspects of recognition essentially reduce to a problem of search. Chapter 6 presents methods for actually enumerating this search space and for combining sources of initial evidence to achieve an efficient ordering for the search. However, as in many problems within artificial intelligence, the size of the search space can quickly become too large for practical enumeration. It is here that the various bottom-up methods for image description can play a vital role. In general, the extent to which a certain type of image description will reduce the size of the search will depend upon the degree to which it is invariant across changes in imaging conditions, such as lighting, viewpoint, or the addition of noise. However, we will argue that one of the most extensively researched aspects of invariant image description—the derivation of depth information—is not the most promising candidate for reducing the size of this search space, both because it is often not available and because it is of only limited effectiveness in reducing the amount of search. Instead of relying upon depth information, we will propose a central role for the process of perceptual organization, in which groupings are formed directly from the spatial structure of the image.

1.0.2:   Perceptual organization

Perceptual organization refers to a basic capability of the human visual system to derive relevant groupings and structures from an image without prior knowledge of its contents. Other names which have been given to this and related topics include figure-ground phenomena, image segmentation, Gestalt perception, and texture description. The human visual system has a highly developed capability for detecting many classes of patterns and statistically significant arrangements of image elements. For example, people can immediately detect symmetry, clustering, collinearity, parallelism, connectivity, and repetitive textures when shown an otherwise randomly distributed set of image elements. Almost all current computer vision systems lack these perceptual capabilities. A major reason why perceptual organization has not been a focus of computer vision research is probably because these groupings often do not lead immediately to a single physical interpretation. However, as a component of a search-based approach towards recognition, this does not prevent the system from making effective use of the organization—the structures can lead to a dramatic decrease in the search space in spite of some remaining discrete instances of ambiguity. The first few chapters of this book will be largely devoted to the problem of providing an underlying theory for the function and goals of perceptual organization. These results will then be used to derive a number of constraints that all perceptual grouping operations must satisfy in order to be functionally adequate.

Although not historically a focus of the computer vision community, perceptual organization has played a much more central role in the psychological study of human vision. The Gestalt psychologists devised many experiments in the 1920's and 30's that tested the way human subjects subjectively grouped simple line and dot patterns, and there has also been more recent work in measuring many related aspects of human vision. Unfortunately, the psychological explanations given for these phenomena have been primarily descriptive rather than functional, and therefore do not give an adequate theory for the role which perceptual organization plays in the overall functioning of the visual system. By examining perceptual organization within a recognition-based computational framework, we hope not only to improve the capabilities of computer vision systems but also to provide useful explanations for the presence and function of many of these psychological phenomena.

1.0.3: The relationship to psychology

Since there is sometimes an uneasy relationship between research in computer vision and the study of human vision, it is important to be clear about the form that the discussion of psychological results will take in the following chapters. Some researchers within the computer vision community consider the development of machine vision to be quite separate from research into the functioning of human vision. After all, why should we be constrained by the biological solution to a problem? However, this view ignores the fact that biological vision is currently the only indication we have that the general vision problem is even open to solution. Without this proof of feasibility, it is hard to imagine that anyone would even think of attempting to interpret the array of light intensities projected from a scene onto a two-dimensional screen. Biological vision is currently our major source of evidence as to which sources of information can or must be used to solve the various components of the vision problem and how these sources can be combined. It is at this level that most of the psychological evidence will be used in the following pages.

The skepticism can also flow in the reverse direction. Psychologists may wonder how computer scientists with largely pragmatic aims can have anything useful to say about specific biological systems. This is probably best countered by repeating David Marr's description of the different levels of computational explanation in vision [Marr, 1977; Marr, 1982]. At the lowest level of explanation is a description of the hardware implementation, and at this level it would indeed be inappropriate to claim results without specific physiological evidence. At an intermediate level is a description of the representations and algorithms which are used, and at this level psychophysical evidence can often be used. At the highest level of explanation we will have a computational theory that provides a specification of *what* is computed rather than *how* it is computed. Just as there can be many possible hardware implementations for a single algorithm, there can be many algorithms for a single computational specification of a problem. However, these higher levels of explanation provide strong constraints and theoretical building-blocks for examining specific implementations at the lower levels. We will be assuming in the following discussions that both computer and biological vision systems will share solutions at the higher levels of computational specification due to the fact that they face a common problem, and we will focus on functional specification rather than similarities of implementation.

1.1: Two viewpoints on computer vision

The approach that we will be taking differs in some important ways from the dominant tradition of research in computer vision. The analysis of any problem must be carried out within some framework that selects the background assumptions and problem definitions on which the work will be built. The following sections will describe two somewhat different conceptions of the problems to be solved in computer vision. The first viewpoint assumes that the primary function of different components of the visual system is to produce disambiguated intermediate levels of representation that represent physical properties of the scene, and that these are in turn further disambiguated by processes leading to higher level representations. This conception differs in some fundamental respects from the recognition-based approach taken in this book, which uses the intermediate descriptions to assist general search procedures in achieving correspondence with prior expectations. While there is clearly a role for both types of process, there is much room for debate regarding the relative importance of these processes in typical visual situations.

1.1.1: Production of disambiguated representations

It is common for researchers in computer vision to point out that any local measurement in the image is the convolution of many different properties of the scene, such as lighting, reflectance, viewpoint, and surface shape. A major focus of computer vision

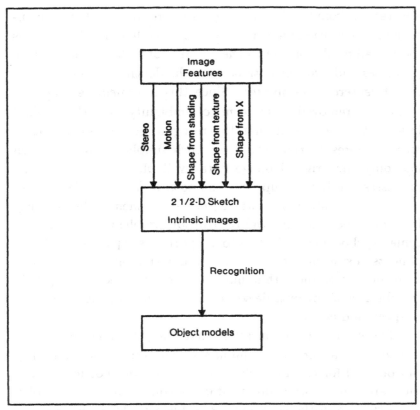

Figure 1-1: A commonly-adopted model for visual recognition assumes that multiple processes operate to derive depth information and other intrinsic physical characteristics from features of the image. These results are combined in intermediate representations such as the $2\frac{1}{2}$-D sketch or intrinsic images. The recognition process then operates from these disambiguated intermediate representations.

research has been to develop processes that can recover some of these intrinsic physical properties of the scene directly from its images. One of the most successful and intensively studied aspects of this project has been the development of methods for recovering depth information. The diagram in Figure 1-1 illustrates a popular model for the visual system, in which multiple processes operate on the image to produce depth information.

The results from the different processes are combined into a common representation known as the $2\frac{1}{2}$-D sketch [Marr, 1982]. This model can be elaborated by the addition of surface-interpolation processes and transformations from the depth representation to object-centered coordinates. Since this intermediate representation has removed many forms of ambiguity from the original image, it is presumed that the recognition process operating on this representation would be much simpler than one which had only the original image data available. Since the initial processes are bottom-up and lead to a useful, well-defined intermediate result, work has proceeded on them independently from any need to solve the recognition problem. There is also some psychological evidence to support this separation of components: experiments with random-dot stereograms or motion correspondence show that human vision can recover depth in the absence of any outside sources of evidence, albeit with a loss of speed and accuracy.

There can be no question that the processes for depth-recovery are a part of the human visual system and that they can be vital for certain tasks. However, it does not follow that these are a necessary component of recognition or that they play a central role in the common visual tasks of daily life. We will argue in particular that depth information is not necessary for recognition, that it is quite often unavailable, and that it is of only limited use for recognition when it is available. The fact that depth information is unnecessary for recognition will be demonstrated in the following chapters by developing methods for achieving recognition directly from two-dimensional image data. It would also follow from the conclusion that depth information is often unavailable to the human visual system in situations where recognition remains easy. There are in fact strict limitations on the applicability of the various proposed processes for recovering depth information. Stereo is useful only when the object is close enough to cause sufficient disparity and is within the restricted boundaries defined by the fusional area of the visual field. Motion requires an elapsed time interval depending upon the relative velocity of the motion, which means that only in the fastest cases of motion will it be of use for immediate recognition. For stationary objects, we must rely on motion by the observer, which at typical rates of human motion is again only of use for nearby objects. The processes for recovering depth from shading and texture gradients make even more specialized assumptions. They seem to apply only to regions that have approximately uniform reflectance or texture, and even then return what can best be described as qualitative constraints on shape rather than quantitative depth information. The function of the $2\frac{1}{2}$-D sketch is to combine these various sources of information so that one source can make up for missing information from the others. However, there are many common situations in which even the combination of these sources would seem unable to provide much quantitative depth information. These situations include objects that are distant, objects that are quickly identified in peripheral vision, two-dimensional pictures of objects, and line drawings. Significantly, there seems to be little degradation in the speed or accuracy of recognition in these situations by human vision.

But in those situations in which depth information is available, isn't it extremely useful? This is clearly true in some situations, such as when encountering a completely unfamiliar object or when performing motor or navigation tasks that require precise three-dimensional information. However, the value is much less obvious for the common visual task of recognition (from which we can usually also derive approximate location in depth). Given that we are basing recognition upon spatial correspondence, it would seem reasonable to consider correspondence in three dimensions rather than just basing it on the locations of two-dimensional image features. However, even when depth measurements are available from stereo or motion correspondence, their accuracy and density are usually lower than those for the locations of features in the image, partly because they are derivative from these two-dimensional measurements. Therefore, from an information-theoretic point of view, the depth information usually provides fewer bits of information than the measurements in the other two dimensions. So, for the task of verifying correspondence with prior knowledge, the addition of depth information can not be expected to provide a major increment to our reliability of verification (of course, as with any source of new information regarding the image, there will be some problems for which it is needed to make a crucial discrimination). There may be ways to use depth information to greatly speed the search for correspondence with prior knowledge, but there is currently no strong evidence for this conclusion. Even complete, accurate depth information, such as that produced by a laser rangefinder, has not been shown to greatly ease recognition. The successful use of two-dimensional perceptual organization may be capable of exploiting most of the useful information.

1.1.2: Searching for spatial correspondence

Figure 1-2 presents a model for visual recognition that contains pathways other than those leading through depth and surface representations. Perceptual groupings can be formed directly from the two dimensional image features and can be used as input to a search-based recognition process. The verification of interpretations can also bypass the need for a depth representation by directly checking the consistency of spatial correspondence between three-dimensional knowledge and the two-dimensional locations of image features. Of course, the capability for forming depth representations is retained when available, but it is no longer the only pathway to recognition. Perceptual groupings can also be formed in three-dimensions from the depth representation, and there is a process of 3-D inference which can infer constraints on depth directly from the two-dimensional perceptual groupings.

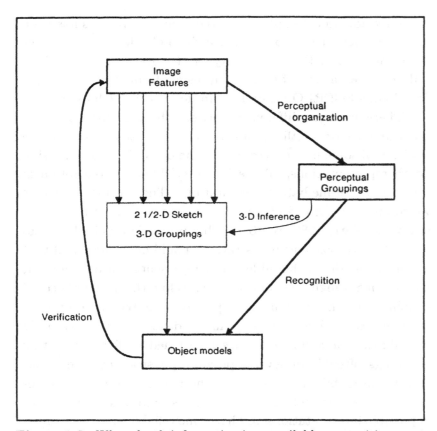

Figure 1-2: When depth information is unavailable, recognition must be achieved through alternate pathways. In this model, a process of perceptual organization results in the formation of perceptual groupings. These can in turn be used directly for generating hypothesized correspondences for recognition. The verification procedure can also operate directly between prior three-dimensional knowledge and the two-dimensional image. The processes for depth recovery remain, but are no longer a necessary part of recognition.

Different chapters of this book will be devoted to developing each of these additional capabilities, including perceptual organization, 3-D inference from perceptual groupings, search-based recognition, and spatial verification. Fortunately, there has already been important previous work in some of these areas, particularly search-based recognition. While these problems have certainly not been completely solved, enough progress has been made on each of the topics to convincingly demonstrate their performance and the practicality of the overall system. Partial implementations of these components form the basis for the functioning SCERPO vision system described in Chapter 8.

There are more differences between this search-based viewpoint and the one outlined in the previous section than just the addition of some new processes and the capability for bypassing depth representations. There is a very different conception of the role of intermediate representations. The contrast is clear if we compare it, for example, with Marr's principle of least commitment [Marr, 1982, p. 106]. This principle explicitly states that a hypothesize-and-test strategy should be avoided and that a conclusion should be added to a representation only after it has reached a high level of certainty. While this principle could simplify the construction of completely disambiguated intermediate representations, it ignores any evidence which is inherently probabilistic or ambiguous. As mentioned earlier, perceptual groupings often have several possible physical interpretations and are probabilistic in nature. Therefore, they only fit comfortably into a model which allows for search among a number of possible interpretations and has some reliable method for final verification.

There is a common unfounded belief that can lead people to prefer the idea of complete depth and surface representations over the use of sparser spatial information. The examples we will be using will be very similar to the problem of interpreting line-drawings since they place primary emphasis on the position of line or point discontinuities in intensity. However, many people consider the problem of interpreting line-drawings to be artificial, and they may have heard anecdotal stories suggesting that people from primitive cultures are unable to recognize such drawings. However, this belief is just not supported by the evidence. A seemingly definitive experiment on this question is described in [Hochberg & Brooks, 1962]. In this experiment, a

Figure 1-3: [Hochberg & Brooks, 1962] describe an experiment in which a child was raised until the age of 19 months without being shown pictures of any kind. Yet, the child had no difficulty in naming the contents of the first line-drawings he saw, which are shown above. This experiment seems to clearly demonstrate that the recognition of line-drawings does not require any special form of learning and that it follows naturally from the ability to recognize three-dimensional objects. [Copyright 1962 by the Univeristy of Illinois Press. Reprinted with permission.]

human baby was raised until the age of 19 months under the constant supervision of his parents who avoided exposing the child to line-drawings or two-dimensional pictures of any kind. Although the baby accidentally had opportunities to glance at some pictures on a few occasions, at no point was the content of a picture ever named to him or was other attention drawn to it. All of the baby's playthings were chosen so that they had solid coloring and no two-dimensional patterning of any kind. Finally, at the age of 19 months the child was shown some line-drawings for the first time, including those shown in Figure 1-3. The child was immediately able to recognize the objects in these drawings, and performed equally well when identifying the contents of black-and-white photographs. This experiment would seem to provide a very strong result that applies to all cultures.

1.2: A demonstration of perceptual organization

The reader may still be unconvinced of the importance of perceptual organization for typical instances of recognition. However, we can demonstrate that the formation of perceptual groupings is prerequisite to recognition by performing the obvious psychophysical experiment of creating an image in which the information necessary for perceptual organization is missing. In Figure 1-4, we have created a drawing of a bicycle that is more than 50% complete, but which has been constructed so that most opportunities for bottom-up grouping having been eliminated (e.g., we have eliminated most instances of significant collinearity, endpoint proximity, parallelism, and symmetry). In informal experiments, this drawing proved to be remarkably difficult to recognize when the subject had no knowledge regarding the identity of the object. In one group of 10 subjects, nine of the people were unable to identify the object within a 60 second time limit, and the tenth person took about 45 seconds. Note that this is in spite of the fact that the object level segmentation has already been performed—the task would be even more difficult if the bicycle were embedded in a normal scene containing many surrounding features. Just in itself, this part of the experiment illustrates the limited capability of human vision for achieving recognition without perceptual organization.

The experiment can be taken one step further by gradually introducing the capability for performing perceptual groupings and seeing whether this decreases the average recognition times. In Figure 1-5 we have added just a single segment to the drawing in 1-4. The added segment was placed at a strategic location that allows it to be combined with other segments in a curvilinear grouping. The recognition times for this second figure were dramatically lower than for the first, with 3 out of 10 subjects recognizing it within 5 seconds and 7 out of 10 within the 60 second limit. Presumably, if the added segment had been placed at

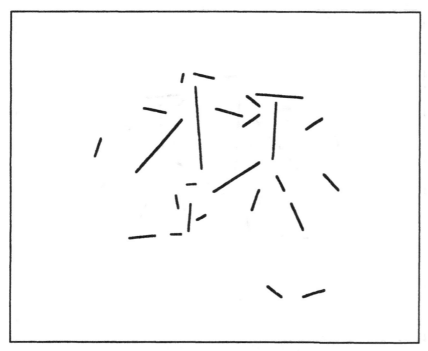

Figure 1-4: When opportunities for bottom-up grouping of image features have been removed, as in the line drawing of a bicycle above, the drawing is remarkably difficult to recognize. The average recognition time for this drawing was over one minute when subjects had no prior knowledge of the object's identity.

some location which did not lend itself to perceptual groupings, the change in recognition times would have been negligible. The final recognition of this figure is clearly based upon achieving spatial correspondence with a single viewpoint of some known object—for example, there is no potential for forming a bottom-up representation at the level of a $2\frac{1}{2}$-D sketch. The ability to influence recognition times by controlling the formation of perceptual groupings illustrates the search-based nature of this process. One can imagine performing a series of these experiments, in which different groupings are introduced, which would allow the experimenter to determine the relative importance of various groupings in accessing a particular object model.

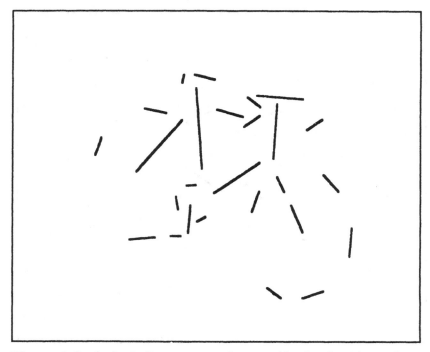

Figure 1-5: A single line segment that provides local evidence for a curvilinear grouping was added to the drawing on the previous page. The average recognition times for this new drawing were greatly reduced as compared to the previous version.

The search-based nature of the matching process can also be demonstrated by introducing non-visual forms of contextual information which reduce recognition times by limiting the set of candidate objects. This was a component of an experiment described in [Leeper, 1935], in which subjects were asked to identify degraded drawings of common objects. One group of subjects was told nothing about the identity of the objects, but a second group was given vague non-visual verbal descriptions of the object class, such as "a musical instrument" or "a means of transportation." These verbal descriptions led to a significant decrease in the amount of time required for recognition. Since these descriptions could have applied to a wide range of visually dissimilar objects, it seems that the best explanation for their influence must be in narrowing the search at the level of object recognition rather than influencing bottom-up descriptive processes or leading directly to the one correct answer. A number of other psychological studies in the area of perceptual organization will be reviewed in the next chapter.

1.3:   Specific functions of perceptual organization

Current knowledge-based vision systems [Roberts, 1966; Shirai, 1978; Brooks, 1981; Goad, 1983] are limited in practice to the consideration of only a few well-specified objects by the sheer size of the search space that must be explored. The model of recognition that we have presented assigns a central role to perceptual organization as a way of reducing the size of this search. Here we will examine some of the mechanisms through which this reduction in search can be accomplished. By understanding these mechanisms, we will be specifying some of the particular functions which perceptual organization can perform in a complete vision system, and we will use these results in later chapters to determine particular attributes of algorithms that carry out the grouping processes. Following are three of the most important functions of perceptual organization:

1) Segmentation: A major reduction in the search space can be achieved by segmentation—the division of the image into sets of related features. Without segmentation, a model would have to be matched against all possible combinations of features in the image, so good segmentation is crucial for reducing the combinatorics of this search. Segmentation has long been recognized as a central problem, but previous methods have been based on region analysis or scene-specific measures rather than on general methods of perceptual organization.

2) Three-space inference: Perceptual organization results in the formation of two-dimensional relations between image features, and these relations can then lead to specific three-dimensional interpretations as described in Chapter 5. For example, collinear lines in the image can be expected to be collinear in three-dimensions unless there has been an unusual accident in viewpoint. In this way, perceptual organization can lead to constraints on depth, which can provide segmentation in three dimensions as well as two.

3) Indexing world knowledge: Given a large database of world knowledge, the most significant factor determining the size of the search space is likely to be the selection of the appropriate object out of the extensive set of possibilities. To the extent that the relations formed by perceptual organization are stable under different viewpoints and imaging conditions, they can be used as reliable index terms to access the body of world knowledge. Each relation will typically have several parameters of variation whose relative values in the image can be used for indexing. For example, collinear line segments can be characterized in a viewpoint-independent manner by the relative sizes of the segments and gaps.

It is important to note that each of these mechanisms for reducing search is based upon the assumption that the relations produced by perceptual organization are the result of regularities in the objects being viewed. This means that any relations which arise through some accident of viewpoint or position are of no use for recognition and will only confuse the interpretation process. This fact will provide the basic method for evaluating the usefulness of specific image relations—relations are useful only to the extent that they are unlikely to have arisen by accident. One of the major goals of our algorithms for perceptual organization will be to statistically distinguish accidental from non-accidental instances of a relation. This goal will form a basis for the further development of methods for perceptual organization in Chapter 3, following a review of some of the previous research on perceptual organization in Chapter 2.

Chapter 2

PREVIOUS RESEARCH
ON PERCEPTUAL
ORGANIZATION

THE HISTORY of research on perceptual organization consists, in its broad outlines, of a search for some underlying principle which would unify the various grouping phenomena of human perception. The Gestalt psychologists thought that this underlying principle was some basic ability of the human mind to proceed from the whole to the part. Later research summarized many of the Gestaltists' results with the observation that people seem to perceive the simplest possible interpretation for any given data—although simplicity proved to be very difficult to define or quantify. The research described in this book is based on the still more recent principle that it is the degree of non-accidentalness that determines the significance of a grouping. In other words, it is not simplicity itself that determines significance but the extent of *surprising* simplicity given expectations regarding the distribution of features.

In addition to this grand search for a single principle, there have been a number of basic psychophysical studies on grouping

processes as well as many attempts to implement specific grouping operations in computer vision systems. While it would be
impossible to cover all of this work in a single chapter, we will
attempt to cover some of the major highlights.

2.1: Gestalt psychology and perceptual organization

In many ways, the heyday for the study of perceptual organization was during the 1920's and 30's. During this period, Gestalt
theory dominated the study of perception, and the study of
perceptual grouping phenomena was a major component of the
Gestalt program. The word *Gestalt* itself means "whole" or
"configuration," and the major goal of the Gestaltists was to
show that perception was something that happened as a whole
rather than as a combination of individual primitive features.

The major contribution of Gestalt psychology to our current understanding of perceptual organization was to develop
a large number of demonstrations of grouping phenomena and
to roughly categorize them into several groups. Figure 2-1 illustrates some of these categorizations as developed by Max
Wertheimer [Wertheimer, 1923], who is recognized as the found-
er of the Gestalt school. These categories can be summarized as follows: (1) *Proximity*—elements that are closer together tend to be grouped together; (2) *Similarity*—elements
that are similar in physical attributes, such as color, orientation
or size, are grouped together; (3) *Continuation*—elements that
lie along a common line or smooth curve are grouped together;
(4) *Closure*—there is a tendency for curves to be completed so
that they form enclosed regions; (5) *Symmetry*—any elements
that are bilaterally symmetric about some axis are grouped together; and (6) *Familiarity*—elements are grouped together if
we are used to seeing them together. Naturally enough, given
such extremely general terms as similarity or familiarity, it was
very difficult to derive any type of quantitative theory. There
were many attempts to put these various grouping tendencies in

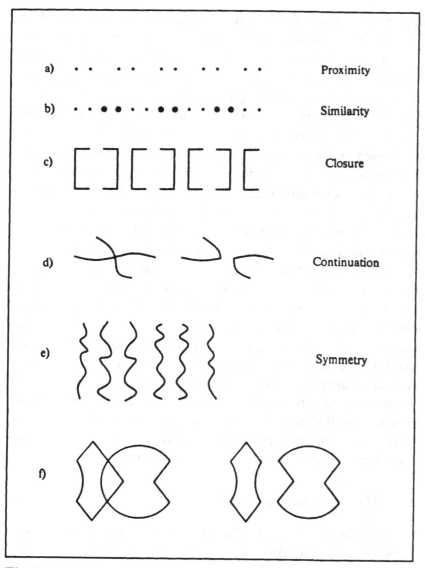

Figure 2-1: These are examples from some of the categories of grouping phenomena developed by the Gestaltists: (a) dots are paired on the basis of proximity; (b) dots are paired based on similarity in size; (c) shapes are grouped as squares due to closure (or continuation); (d) lines are seen as crossing due to good continuation; (e) bilaterally symmetric pairs of lines are grouped; and (f) this example, from [Kanizsa, 1979], illustrates that continuation can override the influence of symmetry.

opposition to one another and see which was stronger, but there were too many variables to come up with a quantitative theory.

Unfortunately, the Gestaltists extrapolated from simple experiments, such as the ones described above, to highly speculative assumptions regarding the overall structure of the brain and mind. They rejected the idea of independent receptors with specific nerve energies and considered the study of sensory psychophysics to be artificial and irrelevant. Instead they built theories based upon "field theory" and the resulting "attractive forces" between components of a perception. In the same way that every minor event in an electromagnetic field is related to every other event in the field, it was assumed that the response of each individual receptor was determined by the overall structure of the perception. This did not stop with the study of perception, but was considered to apply to the entire area of the self and to relationships between the self and the environment. Gestalt psychology also claimed success in "refuting the machine theory of the organism" [Katz, 1950, p. 50], in particular the idea that ordered perceptions arise from the ordered structures and pathways of the nervous system. Eventually, after two decades of prominence, there was the inevitable backlash against Gestalt theory, with the unfortunate side effect that the study of perceptual organization became associated with some of the less scientific aspects of the Gestalt revolution.

2.2: The principle of simplicity

The most important lasting impact of the Gestalt study of perception was that it stimulated many individuals to try to come up with some underlying principle of organization. The original Gestaltists themselves were not very successful at this. They summarized their laws of organization with the single "law" of *Prägnanz,* which just means "goodness of form"—a circularly-defined term with no quantitative formulation. Many psychologists realized that this was unsatisfactory, and by the 1950's there was some agreement on a general principle of simplicity, also known as the "minimum principle" [Hochberg, 1957]. This was stated as the principle that "other things equal, that perceptual response to a stimulus will be obtained which requires the least amount of information to specify" [Hochberg, 1957, p. 83].

Unfortunately, the idea of simplicity is also not well-defined, since the degree of simplicity with which a figure can be described depends entirely upon the description language that is used. However, it seemed that for some reasonable choices of such a language, the simplicity criteria provided an accurate, computable determination of which perception would be perceived. The idea merged nicely with a surge of interest in information theory during the 1950's, since information theory dealt with minimum-length encodings for transmission of information. [Attneave, 1954] took this idea literally, and looked at various particular minimum length descriptions for images or curves and showed that they seemed to correspond to some simple aspects of perception. There have been some recent attempts to define particular languages for describing certain restricted classes of patterns [Leeuwenberg & Buffart, 1983], and to use these to make quantitative predictions for which structures are most likely to be perceived based upon the minimum-parameter specification of the pattern within these languages. Unfortunately, information theory itself provides no specific guidance for selecting the appropriate language of description.

A major limitation of these simplicity arguments is that they assume that the description language will perfectly encode the image. In realistic scenes, any visual pattern is likely to only approximate whatever ideal description is being considered. Presumably there is some trade-off in degree of approximation to the ideal and the strength of the percept, but the simplicity criteria say nothing about exactly what this trade-off will be and how the degree of approximation is measured. This is an example of a problem that is of crucial importance for computer vision and for most real images, but which can be conveniently ignored when setting up idealized, forced-choice experiments in the perception laboratory. Methods for approaching this problem of measuring degrees of approximation, through the use of statistical evidence and prior expectations regarding distributions of features, will be a major topic of this book.

2.3: Grouping as the formation of causal relations

In a recent paper, [Witkin & Tenenbaum, 1983] examine the role that grouping phenomena can play in both biological and computer vision systems. They point out that many current areas of active research in computer vision—such as structure from motion or stereo—are essentially grouping problems in which elements in the image are grouped into sets of related features. Of even greater potential importance is the human capability to derive structure and organization directly from collections of two-dimensional image features. These groupings can be formed without any high-level knowledge of the content of the scene, and it is remarkable that even after the scene has been recognized and understood, the same groupings are nearly always present in the final description. This then provides the clue for the role that these groupings play in vision: the groupings establish causal relationships between elements of the image that are likely to survive intact through later stages of interpretation. In fact, Witkin and Tenenbaum claim that much of the later interpretation process merely consists of attaching labels to these primitive groupings, so that the computationally-intensive work of deriving structure from the image will have been already accomplished by the grouping process.

Given that the goal of the grouping process is to uncover causal relationships between image features, what does this tell us about how to go about the grouping process itself? Witkin and Tenenbaum review a number of criteria that have been used previously in computer vision, such as a desire for economy of representation or *a priori* expectations that smooth descriptions are more likely than complex ones. Their conclusion is that the strength of the most successful methods comes not from the strength of their *a priori* expectations for the grouping but rather from a non-accidentalness argument. In other words, it is the degree to which some relation is unlikely to have arisen by accident which is the most important contributor to its significance. For example, if two parallel curves are considered to be highly significant, it is not due to the fact that structures which project to parallel curves in the image are a more common occurrence than structures which do not, but rather to the very small probability that two curves would happen to be parallel by accident. Of course, it is also true that any other exactly specified relation between two curves would be very unlikely to happen by accident, so the non-accidentalness argument is still relying on *a priori* expectations. However, the most important consideration is not the expectation for parallels versus non-parallels, but rather the expectation for parallels arising by accident from some expected distribution of the constituent features. Given sufficiently tight constraints for an expectation, we can have a very high level of confidence after identifying it even if our prior expectations for it are low. In other words, we can shift our attention from finding properties with high prior expectations to those that are sufficiently constrained to be detectable among a realistic distribution of accidentals.

Of course, the non-accidentalness argument—based essentially on conditional probabilities—does not originate with Witkin and Tenenbaum. As they point out, previous research in computer vision has used it for a number of individual problems [Lowe & Binford, 1981; Stevens, 1981; Ullman, 1979]. However, Witkin and Tenenbaum argue that this is more than a technique that can be applied to a number of individual problems, but is in fact the general goal of image organization. Even when we do not know the ultimate interpretation for some grouping and therefore its particular *a priori* expectation, we can judge it to be significant based on the non-accidentalness criteria.

While this de-emphasizes the role of prior probabilities, it certainly does not eliminate them. There is still the important issue of selecting the set of well-constrained image relations against which the likelihood of non-accidentalness will be judged. Witkin and Tenenbaum suggest the use of spatiotemporal regularity and "fuzzy" identity over space and time. In other words, the class of relations we should be looking for are those which result when one shape is transformed into another using simple image transformations (e.g., translation, rotation, scaling). This is similar to the suggestion by [Palmer, 1983] that organization is performed over the group of Euclidean similarity transformations. However, this set seems to be much too inclusive to account for normal human performance (e.g., people are not very good at grouping rotated instances of a shape or grouping elements which are widely spaced in an image), and it says little about how to judge approximate instances of a relation. One of the aims of this book will be to provide more detailed criteria for selecting this set of significant image relations.

2.4: The role of grouping in computer vision systems

Although many computer vision programs have incorporated aspects of perceptual organization—such as the detection of straightness or collinearity—the use of each relation has typically been approached in isolation and has not been based on general goals or expectations that could apply to all types of images. One of the most general proposals for the use of perceptual organization in computer vision systems was Marr's initial work on the primal sketch. In his paper on early visual processing [Marr, 1976], he developed the idea that the primal sketch should contain not only representations of the discontinuities in intensity, but also various groupings of curves and tokens into larger structures. These groupings would be based on a representation for individual features, called place tokens, that would represent the perceptually salient aspects of each image feature. Marr suggested groupings on the basis of curvilinearity and a process he named theta-aggregation, which groups lines on the basis of parallelism and collinear displacements. He also suggested performing texture description on the basis of peaks in histograms of five different properties of the place tokens: intensity, size, density, orientation, and separations. These texture measures would have to be calculated within each region of the image for various region sizes. Unfortunately, the grouping aspect of the primal sketch was never developed in detail, and received less emphasis in Marr's later work [Marr, 1982].

The particular grouping process that has received the most attention in computer vision is that of clustering collinear points or lines. One popular candidate for carrying out this process has been the Hough transform [Duda & Hart, 1972], which reparameterizes Cartesian space so that points which lie along the same line will have the same coordinates. By transforming all points in this way and looking for clusters which lie at the same location in transformed space, it is possible to search efficiently for all sets of collinear points. Unfortunately, this method is *too* successful in the sense that it entirely ignores proximity in the image. It will group points from widely separated regions of an image which happen to lie close to a common line, while at the same time failing to ascribe significance to points which are close in proximity but not as close a fit to a line. This is in strong disagreement with human performance in collinearity grouping, which places a strong emphasis on proximity. A more psychologically valid approach is described by [Zucker, 1983], who has carried out some psychophysical experiments on the grouping of dots into curvilinear and oriented structures, and proposes a computational model based upon cooperative processing that agrees with these experimental results.

Another grouping process that has received a significant degree of interest is the detection of bilateral symmetry. A number of psychophysical experiments have been carried out to measure the human capability to detect symmetry in random dot patterns [Bruce & Morgan, 1975; Barlow & Reeves, 1979]. These have found that human vision is able to detect symmetry in brief exposures to patterns even after they have been degraded with missing or perturbed elements to a surprising degree. [Brady, 1983] describes work on a system for detecting the symmetries of a closed contour using a representation he calls smooth local symmetries.

Of course, there have been a large number of other computer vision systems which carry out some grouping operations as a part of their larger goals. We will review some of them in later chapters when dealing with individual grouping problems. But, in summary, it can safely be stated that the development of perceptual grouping processes within computer vision is at a very early stage of development.

Chapter 3

MEASURING
THE SIGNIFICANCE
OF IMAGE RELATIONS

PERCEPTUAL ORGANIZATION can be viewed as a process that assigns a degree of significance to each potential grouping of image features. Our goal in this chapter will be to take a unified view of the many grouping phenomena by examining the underlying principles for measuring the significance of each grouping. As was described in Chapter 1, perceptual groupings are useful to the extent that they are unlikely to have arisen by accident of viewpoint or position, and therefore are likely to reflect meaningful structure of the scene. Our basic argument will be that certain image relations are carriers of statistical information indicating that they are non-accidental in origin, and that this degree of non-accidentalness forms the basis for assigning degrees of significance. Note that there are an infinite number of different types of relations that could be considered (e.g., "all pairs of straight line segments at N degrees relative orientation," for any given N), and a combinatorial number of sets of elements to consider in any given image. Only a small subset of these possible relations are likely to be of any significance or are worth

Derivation of methods for image organization

1: Calculating the probability of accidentalness
    1.1: Viewpoint invariance conditions
    1.2: Prior knowledge of probability of occurrence
    1.3: Null hypothesis of position independence
    1.4: Ratio of background density to proximity
    1.5: Recursive application of structuring

2: Limiting computational complexity
    2.1: Local neighborhood calculations
    2.2: Texture characterizations

Figure 3-1: This chapter, as outlined above, attempts to derive the classes of image relations that are most useful for recognition. The value of a relation for the process of recognition depends upon the probability that it is non-accidental in origin and upon the ability to detect it without undue computational complexity.

the effort required for detection. This chapter will examine the many factors that limit this large class of potential relations to the small set of perceptually significant groupings.

Figure 3-1 lists the various factors that must be combined to produce an overall derivation of the set of significant relations. There are basically three problems to be tackled. The first is to derive the classes of relations (e.g., "parallelism" or "collinearity") that should be tested for significance. The second problem is to include probabilistic measures to take into account limitations in accuracy and deviations from the ideal relation (e.g., how significant is the relation between two lines that are within 3 degrees of being parallel and are far apart in the image). The third problem is to limit computational complexity, since some relations are not worth detecting even if they are statistically significant.

From the psychological viewpoint, this chapter could be thought of as a theory for the visual phenomena explored by the Gestalt psychologists. In other words, it attempts to provide a derivation for the classes of spontaneous groupings that would be formed by any visual system that had been optimally designed for recognition. This will not be a theory at the level of mechanism—it does not predict specific physiological structures—but rather a functional theory that makes predictions based upon the assumption that evolutionary design would lead to the optimal functional implementation. It is likely that many different types of mechanisms would be used to implement the various forms of grouping operations, but they should all satisfy the various computational constraints given in this chapter.

3.1: Probability of accidental occurrence

We have divided image relations into two classes: those that arise through an accident of viewpoint or position and those that arise from some meaningful (i.e., predictable) structure in the scene. As was described in Section 1.3, the accidental relations will only interfere with our attempts to match image relations to prior knowledge of objects. This is similar to the point made in [Witkin & Tenenbaum, 1983] when they argue for the use of image relations to uncover the causal structure of a scene. This point will also be supported by the results on model-matching presented in Chapter 6, which show that it is the non-accidentalness of some relation that allows it to reduce the amount of search required during matching.

Therefore, a key to determining which relations are worth detecting and to evaluating their significance is to calculate the probability that they are non-accidental in origin. Many factors enter into this calculation, and they are individually examined in five subsections: (1) knowledge of the image projection process leads us to the conclusion that only certain classes of image relations will occur more often than by chance and will therefore be statistically detectable; (2) statistical estimates of non-accidentalness can also make use of prior knowledge of the probability of occurrence of each relation; (3) the formation of the accidental instances can be modeled by assuming independence of position and orientation; (4) the background density of similar features determines the significance of a given degree of proximity for any relation; and (5) initial relations can recursively be combined into new relations that can influence the original estimates of significance.

3.1.1: Viewpoint invariance conditions

One of the most powerful and general sources of information constraining the image arises from properties of the image projection process which maps a three-dimensional scene into a two-dimensional image. If we make the reasonable assumption that the viewpoint of the camera (or eye) is independent of the objects in the scene, then we can show that only certain classes of image relations are likely to occur more often than by chance. These classes of relations are those that remain stable over a range of viewpoints (e.g., collinearity in the scene projects to collinearity in the image over a wide range of viewpoints). Any mappings that do not remain stable over a substantial fraction of all possible viewpoints will not produce relations in the image that are separable from those arising by chance. For example, lines at right-angles in the scene do not project to lines at right-angles in the image over any significant fraction of the possible viewpoints. Therefore, even if we detect a right-angle in the image, there is no reason to believe that it is anything other than the result of an accidental interaction between viewpoint and some unknown three-dimensional angle.

Figure 3-2 contrasts examples of relations that are significant against those that are not. It is worth pointing out a common misunderstanding that occurs when interpreting figures such as these that illustrate image relations. It is important to remember that *the figures themselves are three-dimensional objects,* and are merely representations of the two dimensional

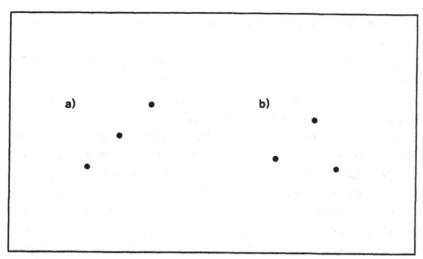

Figure 3-2: Only certain classes of image relations are present over a significant range of viewpoints and therefore will occur more often than by chance. In (a), the three dots form two different types of significant relations, since both collinearity and equal spacings of collinear objects remain invariant over a wide range of viewpoints. However, in (b), the equilateral triangle formed by the three dots can project to any type of triangular relationship in the image depending upon viewpoint, and therefore fails to lead to a significant or detectable image relation for that particular property.

projection onto a retina. So a person will often remark that they immediately perceive the three points in Figure 3-2 (b) as forming an equilateral triangle, forgetting that these points do not project to an equilateral triangle on the retina unless the page is carefully held normal to the line of sight. Therefore, the formation of the perception of an equilateral triangle can come only after determining the three-dimensional locations of the points—for example, by using the knowledge that the page is planar and using the locations of the figure boundaries. Although we will briefly discuss these three-dimensional groupings in later chapters, they occur at a much later stage of visual processing and are qualitatively different in many ways from the initial image groupings that are the topic of this chapter. It is difficult or impossible to introspectively distinguish between the image level of organization and many other forms of visual inference.

The viewpoint-invariance constraint greatly limits the types of relations that can serve as a basis for perceptual organization in the image. There are only a few types of relations, such as collinearity and connectivity, that are preserved over all possible viewpoints. However, there are also a number of other types of relations that are preserved over a wide range of viewpoints and therefore can be expected to arise with substantial frequency. For example, parallelism and the presence of equal spacings between a series of collinear features are properties that are preserved over all viewpoints except where perspective effects are significant. Since many objects occupy only small visual angles or do not extend over a large depth of field in comparison to their distance from the camera, we can still expect these relations to arise frequently in the image. There are yet other relations that require a more careful analysis. For example, constancy of curvature is not strictly preserved under projection (e.g., a circle projects to an ellipse), yet constancy of curvature is largely preserved over local regions of the projected curve covering small radial angles. In spite of these complications, the viewpoint-invariance constraint serves to powerfully limit the infinite set of candidate relations to the small number of spatial properties that are at least partially invariant under projection.

There is another important consequence of the requirement that relations be invariant with respect to viewpoint. The detection of an image relation on the basis that it is unlikely to have arisen through an accident of viewpoint implies that it is likely to be the projection of a specific three-dimensional structure. Therefore, it is possible to infer three-dimensional properties of the scene from the perceptual groupings that are detected in the image. For example, if we decide that an instance of several collinear features in the image is unlikely to be accidental in origin, then we can infer that those features are likely to be collinear in three-space. Chapter 5 will describe a program for inferring constraints on the three-dimensional structure of a scene from perceptual groupings of features in the image. These constraints can be strengthened even further by requiring consistency from the multiple sources of evidence.

3.1.2: Prior knowledge of probability of occurrence

The viewpoint-invariance conditions of the previous section are one of the major factors determining our expectations for the relations that are likely to appear in an image. However, it is also necessary to take into account other sources of prior expectations regarding the contents of an image. We can formalize the role of prior expectations in judging non-accidentalness by making use of conditional probabilities and Bayesian inference. Let $P(r\&a)$ be the probability that both r and a are true, and $P(a|r)$ be the probability that a is true when r is true. Then it follows that:

$$P(r\&a) = P(r)P(a|r) = P(a)P(r|a)$$

Therefore,

$$P(a|r) = \frac{P(a)P(r|a)}{P(r)}$$

This is the basic law of Bayesian statistics. If we let r be the detection of a given image relation to within a certain degree of accuracy, then we can let a be an instance of that relation that arose accidentally and c be an instance that arose for a causal reason. Then $P(r) = P(a) + P(c)$ (since a and c are the two mutually exclusive cases of r) and $P(r|a) = P(r|c) = 1$ (since a and c are instances of r). Therefore, from the Bayesian form above we get:

$$P(a|r) = \frac{P(a)}{P(a) + P(c)}$$

$$P(c|r) = 1 - P(a|r) = 1 - \frac{P(a)}{P(a) + P(c)}$$

These expressions allow us to calculate the probability that a given image relation is non-accidental from the prior probabilities of accidental and non-accidental instances. The following sections will describe ways to estimate the likelihood for the accidental occurrences, $P(a)$. The viewpoint-invariance conditions of the previous section were aimed at selecting those relations that had a significantly high value for $P(c)$, but these are only one component of determining a quantitative estimate for the causal probabilities.

So, how can we determine the prior probability for the causal occurrence of each relation? One reasonable way would be to simply keep statistics of the occurrence of each relation over a suitable sample of images. This empirical approach is a type of learning that might be used in a biological visual system. A more theoretical approach would be to create some general model of the visual world and derive the expected frequencies of the relations from this model.

It is important to realize that these prior probabilities for non-accidental instances of a relation, $P(c)$, need only be order-of-magnitude estimates and that not much hinges on their specific values. By making more accurate measurements in the image (thereby obtaining smaller values for $P(a)$) and combining relations as described in later sections, it is possible to assign causal interpretations to even rarely occuring relations. It is also important to remember that we will only know $P(c)$ for general classes of images, and we don't want our inferences to fail when we are faced with a particular image that has a very different rate of occurrence for that relation. So in practice, prior estimates of $P(c)$ may be more important for selecting which relations to search for than for making inferences during vision. On the other hand, Chapter 6 will show how to make more extensive use of prior probability estimates during later stages of vision.

3.1.3:   Null hypothesis of position independence

As described above, we need to determine the probability that each relation in the image could have arisen by accident, $P(a)$. Naturally, the smaller that this value is, the more likely the relation is to have a causal interpretation. If we had completely accurate image measurements, the probability of accidental occurrence could become vanishingly small. For example, the probability of two image lines being exactly parallel by accident of viewpoint and position is zero. However, in real images there are many factors contributing to limit the accuracy of measurements. Even more important is the fact that we do not want to limit ourselves to perfect instances of each relation in the scene—we want to be able to use the information available from even approximate instances of a relation.

Given an image relation that holds to within some degree of accuracy, we wish to calculate the probability that it could have arisen by accident to within that level of accuracy. This can only be done in the context of some assumption regarding the surrounding distribution of objects, which serves as the null hypothesis against which we judge significance. One of the most general and obvious assumptions we can make is to assume a background of independently positioned objects in three-space, which in turn implies independently positioned projections of the objects in the image. This null hypothesis has much to recommend it; in fact, if we are attempting only to find causal links as suggested by [Witkin & Tenenbaum, 1983] then almost by definition we are looking for any sign of non-independence. There are a number of other properties of vision that lead to modifications of this general assumption, but in practice it forms a strong basis for image segmentation. Most images contain many independent objects that project to nearby locations in the image and a major task of segmentation is to separate them.

Given the assumption of independence in three-space position and orientation, it is easy to calculate the probability that a relation would arise to within a given degree of accuracy by accident. For example, if two straight lines are parallel to within 5 degrees, we can calculate that the chance is only $5/180 = 1/36$ that the relation would have arisen by accident from two independent objects. It should also be noted that the assumption of independence in three-space implies not only position and orientation independence in the image, but also scale independence due to varying distances of objects from the camera. This assumption of scale independence will form a basis for judging significance of similarities in scale.

3.1.4: Ratio of background density to proximity

Our calculations in the previous section were based on the probability that a single, given relation could have arisen accidentally from the independent positioning of its parts. This fails to take into consideration the number of possible relations that are being examined in a given image. These numbers grow according to the square of the number of features being considered—e.g., given only 10 line segments, there are $10 \times (10-1)/2 = 45$ pairs of line segments to be considered. Therefore, given 10 segments, it would hardly be surprising to find two which are parallel within 2 degrees (something that will occur one time in 45 between independently positioned line segments). Figure 3-3 contains an example which illustrates this point.

The result of taking background density into account is that the proximity of the features making up a relation becomes a major factor in judging the relation's significance. As two features come closer together, the expected number of other features within the same proximity decreases sharply for a given surrounding density. Note that proximity is not only a component in judging the significance of all other types of image relations, but is also in itself an important type of image relation

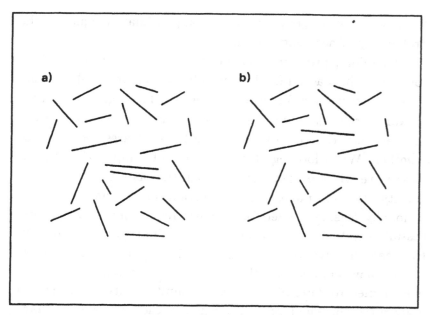

Figure 3-3: The two almost-parallel lines in (a) form a significant relation when they are close together with respect to the background density of similar features. However, as this ratio of proximity to density decreases, the relation becomes less significant, as shown in (b).

that can be used to detect non-accidental groupings. Proximity passes the image invariance test, since features that are close together in three-space will project to features that are close together in the image from all viewpoints (of course, features that are separated in three-space can also project close together in the image due to an accident of viewpoint, which is why the inference depends on the surrounding density of features).

We can specify the results of the interaction of proximity with feature density in more detail. Let d be the density of features in a region and r be the separation of two features from each other. Then the expected number of features $Q(r)$ that would be within r units of a given feature is the density times the area of a circle with radius r:

$$Q(r) = d\pi r^2$$

For low values of $Q(r)$, this will be approximately equal to the probability of accidental occurrence.

Therefore, proximity can be used in isolation or as a factor to take into account when calculating the probability of accidental occurrence for other relations. The significance of a proximity relation is inversely proportional to the square of the separation, and therefore grows rapidly as features become close together. When looking at the problem of computational complexity we will see that feature separation as a function of the density also determines which detection operations are computationally feasible. Therefore a basic requirement for the successful detection of a relation is the proximity of its features in the image relative to the background density of similar features.

We have not specified the size of the surrounding region that is examined to determine the background density of features in a given region. The larger this region is, the more data we have on which to base our statistics; on the other hand, images are not uniform, so the larger the region becomes, the more likely we are to stray into a qualitatively different type of region. There is no easy answer to this question. It seems likely that human vision makes an estimate of feature density only after perceiving inhomogeneities in the feature distribution during texture perception, making this a fairly complicated problem. However, for most images it would produce an adequate answer to merely examine a small region out to two or three diameters of the feature separation.

3.1.5: Recursive application of structuring

Due to limits in the accuracy of image measurements (and possibly also the lack of precise relations in the natural world) the simple relations that have been described often fail to generate the very low probabilities of accidental occurrence that would make them strong sources of evidence for recognition. However, these useful unambiguous results can often arise as a result of combining tentatively-formed relations to create new compound relations that have much lower probabilities of accidental occurrence. For example, we may group a few collinear points into a line which then is found to be part of some larger structure of parallel lines. These later structures provide confirmation for the significance of the earlier groupings. Carrying this process all the way to object recognition, we see how the recognition of the bicycle in Figure 1.4 provided strong confirmation for very tentative groupings formed in the earlier stages of recognition.

The most comprehensive method for combining already-detected relations into new structures is to treat each of the initial relations in the same way as we would a primitive feature. Based on the probability that the relations could have arisen by accident we can calculate the density of occurrence of accidental instances of these relations (making use of the same measurement of the surrounding density of their components as was used for calculating their own significance). We can also take a more empirical approach and examine the surrounding area for other instances of these relations to arrive at a measure of their density, as was done for the initial features. This second approach is preferable where there are other instances of the relations, since it makes fewer assumptions about the prior distribution; however, when there are no other instances, it fails to assign the very low estimates of density that the first approach can assign. Given these density estimates, we can calculate the significance for a compound relation in the same way as for a primitive relation. Since we may be able to assign very low estimates of density to its components, it is possible to assign compound relations much more significance than is possible for those composed only of primitive features.

3.2: Limiting computational complexity

We have outlined a number of factors that determine whether a given image relation could have arisen accidentally. However,

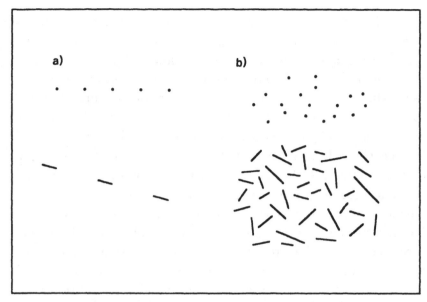

Figure 3-4: The patterns of five equally-spaced collinear dots or three collinear line segments in (a) are not detected spontaneously by human vision if they are surrounded by enough competing line segments, as in (b). This occurs even though the relations remain highly significant in the statistical sense and therefore would likely be of use for segmentation and recognition.

there are cases in which human vision fails to detect groupings that would seem to be highly significant by any reasonable statistical criteria. Some examples are given in Figure 3-4, where the exactly collinear, equally-spaced rows of dots or lines are extremely unlikely to have arisen by accident, yet human vision fails to detect them spontaneously in a surrounding field of similar features. This failure to detect highly significant structures seems to clearly be a limitation of human vision rather than a functional feature. For example, many animal camouflages hide regularities in the animal's structure by surrounding them with nearby spots—a more perfect vision system would not be fooled so easily.

These limitations of human vision are presumably the result of the inherent computational complexity of the grouping processes. It would be computationally intractable to find all possible significant relations in an image, since this would involve examining every possible subset of the image features. One method for limiting this complexity is to only examine groupings which consist of features that are close together in the image, as described in the next section. Another method is to take all the features in a given region and to histogram them according to various properties and look for statistically significant peaks. This is the basis for most texture analysis. Many of the limitations of human performance in segmenting textures [Julesz, 1981; Marr, 1976; Treisman, 1982] can also be ascribed to the computational intractability of looking for peaks in all possible properties in all possible subsets of the image.

It is interesting to note that the problem of computational complexity is an area in which computer vision may substantially outperform biological vision, since computer architectures may be much more flexible in their methods for handling combinatorial problems. For example, it would require very little computation for a computer to notice the significant relations in Figure 3-4 if the appropriate algorithms were used.

3.2.1: Consider only local neighborhoods

Section 3.1.4 described the relationship between the proximity of features and background density when calculating the probability of accidental occurrence. As the ratio of proximity to background density increases, the probability of accidental occurrence decreases by the square of the relative proximity. Therefore, if we are attempting to limit computational complexity we have the most to gain by comparing a feature to its closest neighbors. As features get farther away, it becomes more difficult to distinguish them from accidental occurrences. In addition, features that make up a causal relation are not independently positioned in space, but are often close together. Therefore, the region of the image adjacent to a feature is far more likely to contain another feature which combines with it to form a causal relation than any other region of the same size.

Note that the above arguments are not without exceptions, and it could well be that features that are far apart with respect to the background density could form a significant relation. However, in the interests of limiting complexity, proximity is a very useful basis for limiting the number of comparisons with any feature. As shown by Figure 3-4, this heuristic is apparently adopted strongly by human vision.

It is easy to say that we should only attempt to form relations between a feature and its few closest similar neighbors, but there are many complications in suggesting an actual biological mechanism. At this low level of visual processing, it is likely that all computations are done in parallel by neurons that receive input from only fixed portions of the image. Since our definition of proximity is relative to background density, an implementation must contain many neurons looking for relations at different scales, and only those that contain a limited number of features within their receptive fields would be activated. An example of this type of processing for the detection of collinear dots is presented in [Lowe & Binford, 1982]. Many other authors have also suggested that each feature is only compared to its closest neighbors while searching for relations [Marr, 1982; Stevens, 1978]. A close study of the possible biological implementations for these algorithms would probably go far towards explaining the various strengths and weaknesses of the human capability for detecting image relations.

3.2.2: Texture characterizations

When they refer to "texture description," most researchers mean the use of statistical methods for characterizing sets of features. Whereas the image relations that have been considered so far

deal with only a few features at a time and are highly sensi-
tive to a feature's spatial location, most texture measures treat
an arbitrary number of features within a given region without
concern for their precise location. On the other hand, there is
no precise dividing line between some types of image relations
and some texture description operations—for example, noticing
that a number of edges are parallel to one another in an image
can merge smoothly with the operation of noticing a significant
peak in the distribution of line-segment orientations in that same
region.

Although texture description has become a major topic of
research in its own right, we are placing it under the section
on limiting computational complexity because that is its essential role in comparison with the detection of individual image
relations. Given unlimited amounts of computational power, it
would be most accurate to examine all possible sets of image features for those relations that are most significant with respect
to the surround. However, as the number of elements to be
considered in each set grows, the computational costs increase
rapidly. Texture methods bring this computational cost under
control by ignoring certain parameters of each feature (such as
specific location within the region being examined) and looking
only for peaks in histograms of the remaining properties.

Many different techniques have been tried in experimental
attempts to characterize textures, ranging from Fourier analysis methods to specialized techniques for highly regular textures. The research that is most closely related to the methods
used here is that described in [Marr, 1976; Marr, 1982]. Marr
describes texture operations based upon orientation, length,
width, density, and color. An interesting aspect of these texture
operations are the severe computational limitations of human
texture vision. Marr shows one example in which humans fail
to distinguish a region consisting only of line segments at two
specific orientations from a region of completely random orientations. Once again, this is a case of human vision failing to

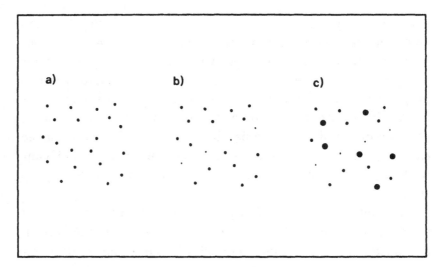

Figure 3-5: The four collinear dots in (a) are not easily detected for the reasons presented in Figure 3-4. However, when they can be segmented on the basis of size in a texture operation, as in (b), the collinearity becomes much easier to detect (it would be useful to run psychophysical experiments with this example to determine whether these effects are perceptually immediate or require scrutiny). Texture segmentation is based on the size of histogram peaks, so if we spread the histogram of size out by increasing the size of some of the larger dots, as in (c), much of the effectiveness of the texture segmentation seems to be lost.

detect a property that is extremely unlikely to have arisen by chance and would therefore likely be of use for recognition. It is also a property that would not be unduly difficult for a computer program to detect.

Texture description serves an important preliminary function for the detection of individual image relations by segmenting out subsets of features with similar properties from a denser background. Whenever a peak is detected in a texture characterization, all those elements that fall under the peak can be treated as an isolated set. Figure 3-5 illustrates how the texture operation can even segment smaller elements from a field of larger ones, and how the segmentation operation can seemingly be disrupted by changing the shape of the distribution.

When we referred in previous sections to the "surrounding distribution of similar elements," the definition of which elements are "similar" probably depends on which elements are grouped together by texture operations. In other words, elements are first segmented according to peaks in histograms of the properties considered by texture description operations, and are then considered in terms of these segmented sets. Therefore, texture description should rightfully be considered an essential aspect of perceptual grouping operations rather than something for merely characterizing sets of elements.

3.3: Conclusions

This chapter has examined many different factors that must be combined to derive the final set of relations that can be detected perceptually in an image. However, we obviously still have a great deal of work ahead to translate these constraints into specific computer algorithms for performing the various grouping operations. One part of this task will be taken up in Chapter 4, where an algorithm will be developed for describing image curves in terms of their most significant structures. Later chapters will develop some other aspects of the perceptual operations. Simple versions of these grouping operations are implemented in the SCERPO vision system described in Chapter 8.

There have been a number of unspecified parameters in the methods presented in this chapter (such as the size of the surrounding region that is considered when measuring feature density). There are two approaches for resolving these uncertainties: theoretical and experimental. Almost all of the discussion so far has been theoretical in that it is derived from basic properties of image formation and from relatively simple models of possible scenes. However, some of the parameters, such as the expected prior distribution of various scene relations, are more easily seen as empirical properties of our world than as theoretical topics for vision researchers. For example, it might be the case that certain aspects of human vision function to overcome specific types of biological camouflage. In cases such as these, any attempts to derive the parameters from detailed scene models could lead the research far afield from the basic topics of computer vision. The most satisfying long-term solution would be to design learning systems that can derive these parameters from their visual input.

Chapter 4

THE SEGMENTATION
OF IMAGE CURVES

In THIS CHAPTER we will apply the methods of perceptual organization to the difficult but important problem of segmenting image curves. Smoothed, segmented image curves are important perceptual structures in themselves, as well as being needed for the subsequent detection of collinearity, parallelism, connectivity, and other perceptual groupings. Most current edge detectors only detect edge points (image locations through which an edge is judged to pass) and possibly link these together into lists of points on the basis of proximity. The gap between the output of edge-detection techniques and the smoothed, segmented curve descriptions needed for model matching and many perceptual grouping operations is a significant missing link in current image-description methodology. One reason for the difficulty of curve segmentation is that it is actually a combination of several different problems: choosing the best scale of description for a curve, deciding where to place tangent discontinuities (corners), and assigning levels of significance to the final segmentations. This chapter will outline the various requirements that an ideal solution to this problem should satisfy, and will demonstrate a computer program that satisfies most of them. The methods we develop for this problem can potentially be applied to many other perceptual problems (such as speech processing) in which significant structures of unknown scale and location must be detected in low-level data.

Most previous approaches in computer vision to producing smooth curves from lists of points have had the goal of smoothing over small deviations in the curve caused by noise and inaccuracies in the imaging process, and thereby recovering the projection of the presumably perfectly smooth curve in the scene. However, this objective is inadequate for the purposes of later grouping operations and greatly understates the capabilities of human vision. A complete curve segmentation method must not rely on any prior estimate of how "noisy" the curves will be, but must find significant curvilinear structure whenever it occurs at any resolution.* This is necessary because objects in the real world do not necessarily have perfectly smooth edges, and we cannot know in advance the degree of roughness they will exhibit. In addition, it is often impossible to have prior estimates of the degree of imaging-induced noise, and these noise properties can vary with local properties of the scene such as the amount of surrounding texture. It is quite possible for a curve to simultaneously exhibit significant curvilinear structures at more than one resolution, as is shown in Figure 4-1. It is necessary to detect structures at all possible resolutions for the purpose of forming further groupings or inference. For example, the segmentation in 4-1(b) is adequate to recognize one instance of collinearity, but other groupings are only apparent when lower resolution structures are recognized as in Figure 4-1(c).

Curve segmentation is an example of a problem for which the Gestalt "simplicity" criteria for segmentation are clearly inadequate. We are not attempting to choose among alternative

---

*We use "resolution" in the context of curve smoothing to refer to the allowed range of transverse deviations of the original points from the smoothed curve description.

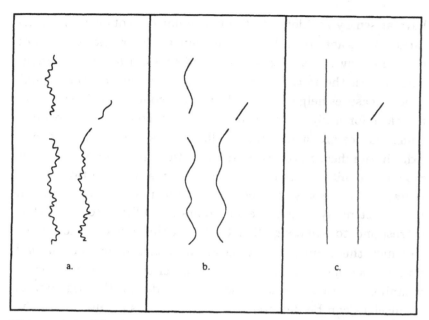

Figure 4-1: The linked lists of edge points in (a) can be segmented at at least two different resolutions of description, as shown in (b) and (c). Although one instance of collinearity can only be detected in (b), the parallelism between the two major segments and the other instance of collinearity can only be detected after recognizing the larger scale structures shown in (c).

exact descriptions for some data, but rather are choosing among an infinite set of possible approximations to the initial input. The "simplest" approximation for any curve would be, say, a straight line. The simplicity criteria do not specify any way to resolve the trade-off between increased simplicity of description and decreased accuracy of approximation to the original data. We will look to the non-accidentalness criteria for measuring significance—in conjunction with the distribution and prior probability estimates described in Chapter 3—to find a method for resolving this trade-off.

As with all the other forms of perceptual organization presented in this book, we will be basing our estimate for the significance of a grouping on the degree to which it is unlikely to have arisen by accident. In the particular case of curve segmentation, we want to find those curvilinear descriptions that are most unlikely to have arisen by accident from noise or random variation in the initial lists of points. Not only do the significance measures help us to decide which resolutions of description to select for a given curve, but they also help us to determine which curves are significant at all. Just as a list of points may exhibit significant structure at more than one resolution, so it may not exhibit significant structure at any resolution. This is important because the edge detection methods currently in use detect many spurious edge points in addition to those that correspond to some significant edge in the image. The degree to which these initial points group into significant longitudinal structures is a strong indicator of whether they have arisen from meaningful structures in the scene. In addition, the edge points themselves can be detected at different scales of filtering of the image, and [Witkin, 1983] provides a complementary method for deciding which points are significant according to their stability across these scales of detection.

4.1: Previous research on curve segmentation

There has been relatively little research into the problem of producing segmented image curves from lists of edge points as compared with the large literature on the detection of the edge points themselves. As already mentioned, most of this work has been based on the goal of simply removing imaging-induced noise. Therefore, these methods perform smoothing at only a single, pre-determined resolution. [Shirai, 1978; Pavlidis, 1977; Rutkowski & Rosenfeld, 1978] all describe methods for smoothing a curve at a single resolution and then assigning points of tangent discontinuity to those places at which curvature is high. [Rutkowski & Rosenfeld, 1978] apply a number of different smoothing and corner-detection methods to the same data, and recommend the use of a simple smoothing technique that measures curvature by looking at the angle between adjacent tangents, where the tangents span some constant number of points on the curve. As the tangents span larger numbers of points, their local variation decreases and they reflect the lower-resolution structure of the curve. Corners are assigned to those points on the curve corresponding to peaks in curvature. [Shirai, 1978] uses a similar technique, and follows it by fitting straight lines and conic sections to the segmented intervals between corners.

Figure 4-2 illustrates the application of a single-resolution smoothing and corner detection algorithm to some actual curve data. This was one of my first attempts to produce a curve segmentation algorithm. The linked lists of edge points were produced by the Marimont edge detector [Marimont, 1982]. These were then smoothed by the method of taking tangents over extended intervals, and corners were assigned to those locations that showed either high curvature or high change in curvature. Points and tangents were then sampled at regular intervals along these curves, and cubic splines were used to draw the final smoothed representation. The final result looks pleasing to the naïve eye, and seems to have removed much of the noise. However, it has failed to actually detect the significant aspects of the curvilinear structure, and these results are hardly any better for further perceptual operations than was the original data. They look good to the eye because the human visual system can still perform all the lower levels of grouping and segmentation; however, these groupings have not been made explicit in the output. For example, if we wanted to do grouping on the basis of collinearity, there are many cases in which the tangents at the endpoints do not reflect the predominant direction of the rest of the curve. More significantly, we have generated no information as to the extent to which a given tangent direction at an endpoint is supported by the rest of the points in that curve. For the purposes of model matching, there are no higher-level descriptions and measures of significance for structures that would

Figure 4-2: The linked edge points at the top were produced by the
Marimont edge detector from an image of a bin of connecting rods. The
smoothed cubic splines at the bottom were the result of the author's
early attempts at a curve segmentation algorithm. Although the results
look pleasing to the eye, they consists only of local approximations to
the original data. Therefore, they fail to detect more global aspects of
the structure or to distinguish between significant and non-significant
structure.

be directly useful for the matching task. It was the shortcom-
ings of this early attempt at curve segmentation that led to the
approach described in the rest of this chapter.

[Hoffman, 1983] reports some recent work on smoothing at
multiple resolutions and selecting the *natural scales* of description. His method examines chords of varying lengths (as in the
methods described above) centered at each point on the curve,
and looks at the variance in the direction of these "smoothed
tangents" with changes in their length. A natural scale is taken
to be one for which the lengths of the tangents can be changed
over a substantial range with comparatively small deviations in
direction. This method is qualitatively superior to the single-
resolution techniques described above, and Hoffman has demonstrated its capability for finding more than one resolution of
description for various synthetic curves. On the other hand,
the method makes no attempts to find corners in curves, and it
does not have any reasoned criteria for determining the degree to
which the resulting descriptions are perceptually significant. In
this chapter we will tackle these problems by using the criterion
of non-accidentalness to measure the significance of particular
segmentations and scales of smoothing.

One goal that has been emphasized by Hoffman and by others working on curve description has been to find the maxima,
zeros, or minima of curvature for the purposes of partitioning the
curve into parts. The most frequently cited sources of evidence
for the salience of these features have been some psychological
experiments described in [Attneave, 1954]. Attneave produced
a drawing of a cat by linking points of maximum curvature with
straight lines, as shown in Figure 4-3, and noted that the resulting drawing retained a strong fidelity to the original picture.
This drawing has been widely reproduced in textbooks on perception and in papers relating to curve segmentation, and has
been said to show that maxima of curvature are the most perceptually significant features of curves. However, as shown in
Figure 4-3(b), if we choose the points that are as far removed

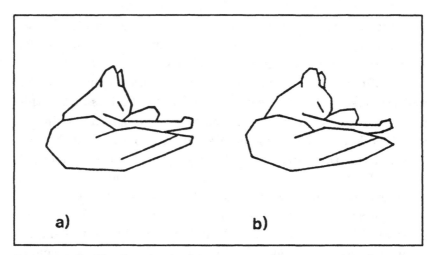

Figure 4-3: The drawing in (a) was created by connecting the points of maximum curvature in a picture of a cat with straight lines, as described in [Attneave, 1954]. The human ability to easily interpret this drawing has been widely cited as evidence for the fact that points of maximum curvature are perceptually significant to human vision. However, if we instead connect points that are shifted half way between the original points of maximum curvature (while leaving curve terminations in place), the drawing in (b) remains highly recognizable and perceptually very similar to the original. Therefore, the locations of the points of maximum curvature can hardly be said to be of great perceptual significance.

as possible from the original points of discontinuity chosen by Attneave, this drawing remains about as recognizable as before the transformation. A contrary hypothesis, derived from the requirements of model-based vision, is that it is the perpendicular proximity of the image curves to the projections of object curves that is most significant. The ability to introduce tangent discontinuities into a smooth curve—at maxima of curvature or elsewhere—without seriously affecting recognition is actually an indication that local values of curvature need not match the predicted curvatures. A second experiment performed by Attneave was to ask subjects to approximate an undulating curved shape with a pattern of 10 dots that would resemble the shape as closely as possible. He discovered that subjects usually placed these dots at points of maximum curvature. However, it is a simple geometric fact that connecting points of maximum curvature with straight lines will cause the resulting lines to lie closer to the original curve than connecting intermediate points, so this hardly constitutes evidence for the perceptual significance of maxima of curvature. A more convincing and theoretically satisfying approach to determining perceptual significance of curve features would be to examine the stability of these features of three-dimensional curves under projection onto the image from different viewpoints. Curve maxima do not have this property of stability, but curvature inflection points, discontinuities in tangent, and curve terminations do remain stable. [Marimont, 1984] analyzes other properties of curves, such as zeros and sign of curvature, for stability under projection and in the presence of noise, and this approach promises to provide far more solid grounds for determining perceptual salience.

4.2:   Significance of a curve segmentation

The theory that the major function of perceptual organization is the detection of non-accidental structure can be used to restate the problem of curve segmentation. Under this theory, a natural description for a curve is one that is unlikely to have arisen by accident. Since the measure of non-accidentalness is in terms of ordinary probabilities, it allows us to determine the trade-offs between differing forms of description, such as different scales of smoothing versus the insertion of corners in the curve description. The major requirement for applying this theory is some way to measure the probability that a sequence of linked points arising from random variation or noise would accidentally happen to match a given type of curve description with the given degree of accuracy. This measure can then be used to select between alternative segmentations or to determine whether a given description is statistically significant rather than accidental.

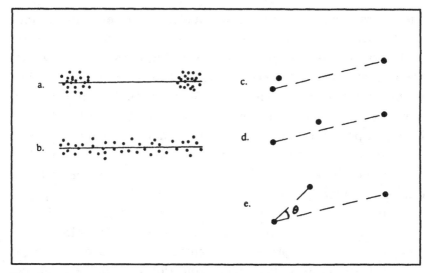

Figure 4-4: The two sets of points in (a) and (b) have the same standard deviations from lines of the same length, yet (b) is much more significant as a linear feature than (a). The points in (a) may be related only by proximity relations, with no necessary significance in terms of linearity. The same situation is illustrated for just three points in (c) and (d), where the third point in (c) may be close to the line joining the other points due only to its proximity to one of the endpoints. Therefore, it is the angle formed by the third point with the line joining the others, as shown in (e), rather than its distance from the line that is measured to determine significance.

Since the edge points will have already been linked on the basis of proximity, we must be careful not to confuse the non-accidentalness in proximity with the measurement of non-accidentalness in curvilinearity. Many of the usual statistical methods for measuring the fit of a set of points to a curve are not useful for this problem because they fail to make this distinction. For example, Figures 4-4(a) and 4-4(b) illustrate the difficulties that arise if we use the common method of comparing the standard deviation of the perpendicular distance of the points from the line with the standard deviation in the direction parallel to the line. As the figure demonstrates, low probabilities of accidental occurrence for this measure may be entirely due to proximity groupings rather than curvilinear ones. Figures 4-4(c) and 4-4(d) illustrate the same point for the simplified case of just three points. Therefore, in this case it is not the perpendicular distance of the central point from the line determined by the other two points that is significant in itself, but rather the probability that this distance is as small as it is given the proximity to the closest defining point of the curve. This measurement effectively factors out the influence of proximity between points in reducing the distance to the curve. In practical terms, the quantity that needs to be measured is the angle between the curve and the vector from the central point to the closest endpoint, as shown in Figure 4-4(e). Since the null hypothesis is that the third point is related to the endpoint only by proximity and not direction, the probability that the magnitude of this angle is less than θ is $2\theta/\pi$.

This method can be extended to cases with more than three points by applying it recursively to the three points with greatest separation and then to each sub-segment between these points. The two points with greatest separation are used to define the straight line, and the point with the greatest minimum distance to these points is chosen as the central point. However, it is not the deviation of this center point from the line that is significant, since there may be other nearby points that are farther from the line but which happened not to be as close to the center of the line. Therefore, the measure of deviation is taken to be the maximum of the deviations of all the points in the linked list. The position of the central point along the curve is still significant, since it determines the degree to which proximity can be discounted as a cause of the perpendicular fit to the line. The measurement is then repeated for each of the two segments between the center point and the endpoints, using the same maximum deviation as was measured for the original segment. Since the linearity of the internal structure of these segments is independent of the original measurement of linearity, these probability values are all multiplied together. The recursion continues until the smaller segments have negligible significance (due to the large transverse deviations with respect to their lengths) or have no more internal points.

The method can also be extended to examine fits to circular arcs in addition to straight lines. This is done by simply fitting a circular arc to the three points in the initial set that are farthest apart, and by looking at the fit of the remaining points relative to their minimum arc distance to these defining points as was done for the straight line case. Although it would be possible to extend this search for structure to still higher order curves (e.g., spirals), it is far from clear that there is much to be gained by looking for significance with respect to these structures or that human vision performs these operations. As more parameters are introduced into the underlying representation, the set of points being tested must become larger or have a substantially better degree of fit in order to have the same statistical significance as for the simpler case. This stage of processing is for the purpose of detecting natural scale and description; after the simpler structures have been detected, other methods can be used to spline them into smooth curves.

Admittedly, the methods described above are not symmetric since they choose certain distinguished points to define the initial curve for fitting. These methods were chosen because they provide a close degree of approximation to the optimal curve, but require very little computation. Computation time is important because the significance measure will be applied numerous times to different portions of each curve. Given the availability of powerful parallel computers, it would be possible to perform least-squares fitting or other forms of optimization. It should again be noted that we are only attempting to measure probabilistic significance of structures rather than produce the final curve descriptions. More significant than the precise measurement of probability are the many qualitative criteria that the methods satisfy, such as the separation of linearity measures from proximity effects. They also take appropriate account of

the number of points that support a curve description: as the
number of points rises, the value returned by the recursive calculation increases until the points are closer than their transverse
deviations from the curve, in which case further points provide
no further support.

4.3: Selecting the most significant structures

Given a method for determining the significance of a curve segment, we would like to divide the initial linked list of points into
segments that have the highest possible significance values. In
the absence of any more immediate technique for achieving this
goal, we will take the exhaustive approach of testing groupings
over all possible scales and positions. It would be too costly to
test every possible segment of the curve for significance. However, if we allow a reasonable margin of error, it is possible to
cover all scales and locations with a relatively small number of
groupings. In the algorithm that has been implemented, we examine groupings at all scales differing by factors of two, from
groupings of only three adjacent points up to groupings the size
of the full length of the curve (amounting to 6 scales for a curve
of 100 points). At each scale, we examine groupings at all locations along the curve, with adjacent groupings overlapping by
50%. This means that any given segment of the curve of any
length will have at least one grouping attempted that covers
50% of its length but does not extend outside its borders. Figure 4-5 illustrates the set of all groupings that are attempted for
a single curve.

The great value of this exhaustive approach is that the decision of where to segment the curve with tangent or curvature
discontinuities can be carried out after the detection of significant curvilinearity rather than before. Previous methods of
curve segmentation have attempted to directly search for locations of tangent discontinuities based upon local measures
of smoothed curvature [Shirai, 1978, Rutkowski & Rosenfeld,

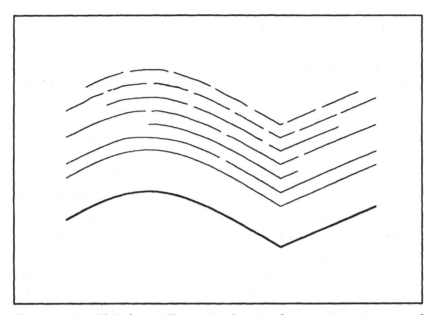

Figure 4-5: This figure illustrates the set of segments at a range of scales and locations that are tested for the single curve shown at the bottom. By testing at scales differing by a factor of 2 and locations overlapping by 50%, any given interval of the original curve will contain one of these segments covering at least half of its length.

1978]. Our approach is the dual—we look for segments of the curve that exhibit significant curvilinearity, and then tangent and curvature discontinuities are assigned to the junctions between neighboring segments. When it is possible to connect neighboring segments without introducing such discontinuities, a spline representation can be used to connect them if natural-looking output is desired.

After measuring the significance of all groupings over the range of scales and locations, a selection procedure is executed to find those groupings that best reflect the significant structure of the curve. In our implementation, any segments that have probabilities of accidental occurrence above a 0.05 threshold are discarded. If all segments of the curve fall above this level, then the curve is considered to exhibit no significant structure (this often occurs when edge points do not result from any underlying physical structure and therefore form curves that wander randomly in the image). Next, a procedure is run which examines the segments at all scales for each point along the curve, and selects only those segments that are locally maximum in significance with respect to scale. It is possible for significance to rise and fall more than once as the range of scales is traversed, in which case more than one scale of segmentation will be chosen. This operation removes the great majority of segments and leaves an average of only one or two segments at each location along the curve; however, due to the greatly differing lengths of the segments, there still remain some segment descriptions that are simply shorter subsets of longer curves that are of similar significance. Therefore, a final comparison is carried out to detect these cases in the remaining segments, so that the shorter subsets can be removed. One segment is considered to be a subset of a longer segment description if its extension to the endpoints of the longer segment remains within the transverse deviation bounds of that segment and its significance squared is less than that of the longer segment.

The operation of deciding whether one segment description can be considered to be a subset of a longer segment description can also be used as a simple method for detecting significant curvilinearity between segments. Two segments can be considered curvilinear and combined to create a new segment if this new segment passes the test for significance and if at least one of the original segments is a subset of the new segment according to the above definition. This satisfies the intuitive criteria that would result if a curved segment were cut by a gap into smaller pieces. Of course, the above test cannot reasonably be applied to all possible pairs of segments in the image, so our implementation first indexes all segments into a multi-dimensional array according to location and endpoint tangent directions. Only those pairs that satisfy a simple first level filter for matching of

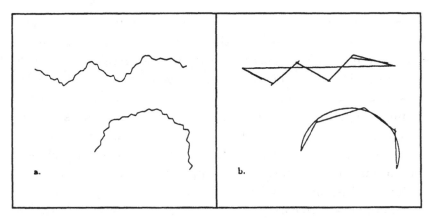

Figure 4-6: The hand-input lists of edge points in (a) have been deliberately drawn so as to have more than one scale of structure. When these are given as data to the curve segmentation algorithm, it returns the segments shown in (b), which make these multiple levels of structure explicit. For example, the top curve can be described as a series of short straight lines or a single roughly linear structure.

location and tangent direction are subject to the detailed test for curvilinearity.

4.4: Demonstration of the algorithm

The algorithm described in the preceding sections has been implemented in MACLISP on a DEC KL-10 computer. It has been tested on a number of synthetic curves, as well as some edge-point lists detected in natural images. Figure 4-6(a) illustrates the application of the algorithm to some hand-drawn lists of edge points that exhibit multiple levels of structure. For example, the lower curve can be viewed as a single circular arc or as a series of straight line segments. When these data are given as input to the curve segmentation program, it returns the segments shown in Figure 4-6(b) that explicitly capture these multiple levels of structure.

A more realistic example is given in Figure 4-7, which demonstrates the application of the algorithm to some edge lists derived from real image data. Figure 4-7(a) shows a small 30 by

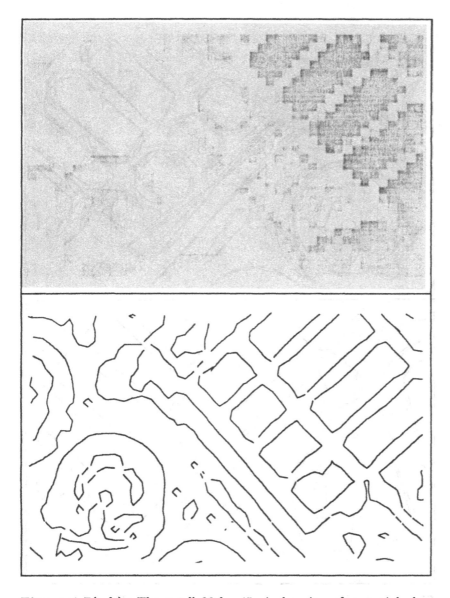

Figure 4-7(a,b): The small 30 by 45 pixel region of an aerial photograph shown in (a) was run through the Marimont edge detector to produce the linked edge points shown in (b). The transverse positions of these edges are interpolated to subpixel accuracy. The goal of the curve segmentation algorithm is to find significant curvilinear structures among these lists of points.

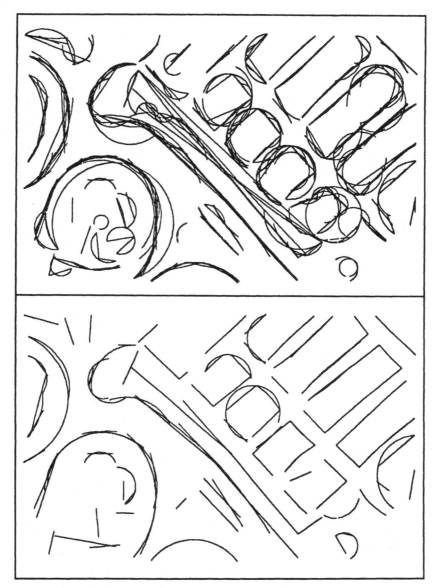

Figure 4-7(c,d): All the segments at different scales and locations
that were tested for significance are shown in (c). A significance threshold was then applied and only those segments that were above this
threshold and were locally maximum in significance at some location
along the curve were retained. The results of this selection process are
shown in (d). Each segment is a straight line or a circular arc.

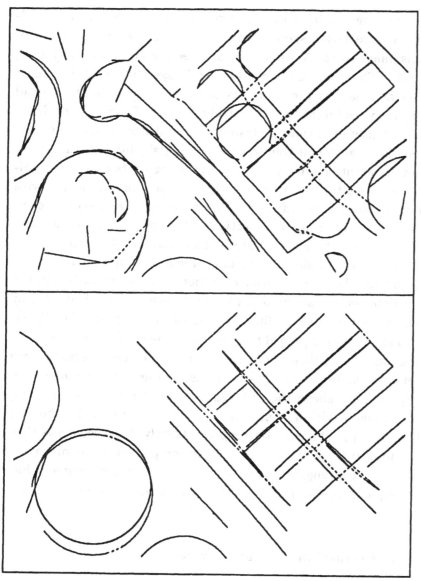

Figure 4-7(e,f): Segments that could be part of the same curvilinear structure are shown in (e) connected by a dashed line. These pairs are then recursively combined into new segments. The final results are shown in (f) with a higher threshold on significance, so that only the most significant image structures are displayed. Compare these results with your perception of (b).

45 pixel region from an aerial photograph of an oil tank facility. Figure 4-7(b) shows some linked edge data generated from this image by the Marimont edge detection program [Marimont, 1982]. This program convolves the image with a filter of fixed size and detects the locations of zero crossings in the second derivative of intensity to subpixel accuracy. Figure 4-7(c) shows all the groupings that are tested for significance at all scales and locations, although the widely differing significance values are not apparent. Figure 4-7(d) shows the segments that remain after selecting those that are locally maximum in significance with respect to scale and after applying the other selection operations described in the previous section. These segments are intended to correspond to the most statistically significant structures embedded in the original individual curve descriptions. Given these segments, the curvilinearity detection methods described in the previous section are used to connect the endpoints of curvilinear segments with dashed lines, as shown in Figure 4-7(e). When two segments are judged to lie on the same curve, a new segment is created from their combination and the original segments are removed unless their significance is greater than this new one. Figure 4-7(f) shows the end result of this process after removing all segments with a significance less than a stricter threshold of 0.01. This final description represents only those segments that are judged to be of exceptionally strong perceptual significance. One of the strengths of this algorithm is that each segment has an explicit significance value that can be used during later computations.

4.5: Evaluation and future research

The algorithm that was demonstrated above has a number of important advantages over other techniques currently being used for curve description. Its major strength is its capability for detecting and evaluating curvilinear structure over a wide range of scales. These structures are assigned significance in inverse

proportion to the likelihood that they could have arisen accidentally. In addition to selecting the most natural scales of
description, they can be used to differentiate edge points that
arose due to structure in the scene from those that are artifacts
of the imaging or edge detection process. Unlike most previous
approaches, the methods can operate in the presence of imaging-
induced noise or random perturbations in the scene without any
prior knowledge of their scale of occurrence.

On the other hand, the algorithm would probably require a
number of extensions and improvements for practical use in a
vision system. The current implementation is not very efficient,
and requires about 20 seconds of computation time on a KL-
10 for even the small region that was demonstrated. However,
since each list is segmented independently, the algorithm could
be implemented in parallel hardware to reduce execution time.
Further work needs to be done on recognizing pairs of segments
that are qualitatively similar, so that some of the duplications
in the final results of the current algorithm can be avoided. The
use of splines to connect adjacent segments into smooth curves
would do much to enhance the display of the final results and
possibly assist later stages of a visual system. Alternatively,
smoothed curve descriptions could be used from the outset as
in [Marimont, 1984], and non-accidentalness could be judged
according to the degree of constancy of curvature relative to the
scale of smoothing.

Possibly the most difficult problem that remains to be solved
is the interaction between multiple scales of curve description
and multiple scales of edge detection. In the demonstration
above, only one high-resolution edge operator was used to detect
edge points, so that any slowly changing variations in intensity
would have remained undetected. It seems unlikely that the
low resolutions of curve segmentation could be run only on the
output of low-resolution edge operators, since this would be ex-
pecting two largely independent physical processes—those that
gave rise to the intensity cross-section of the edge and those that

gave rise to its longitudinal structure—to always operate at the same scales. It would require about 5 times the current amount of computation to examine every curve segmentation at every scale of edge detection—which would hardly be a prohibitive factor—but this still leaves the problem of choosing among the larger number of resulting descriptions. A preliminary selection process operating on the edge descriptions, as in [Witkin, 1983], could also be used to simplify and improve the process of choosing from among the descriptions. Before selecting one of these approaches, it would be very useful to have results from psychophysical experiments that test the capability of the human visual system to detect low-resolution curve segmentations among edge points that in turn can be detected only with high resolution edge operators. In fact, there is a strong need in general for psychophysical data on curve segmentation.

Chapter 5

THE USE OF VIEWPOINT INVARIANCE

CHAPTER 3 described the properties of the image formation process that determine which image groupings will occur significantly more often than by chance. In particular, only those image groupings that are present over a substantial range of viewpoints of a scene will occur often enough to be reliably separated on statistical grounds from accidental occurrences of the same image features. In addition to determining which image groupings are detectable, these viewpoint invariance conditions lead to specific inferences regarding three-space relations from the two-dimensional image groupings. Figure 5-1 illustrates this form of inference, which can provide some of the same three-dimensional information as processes such as stereo or shape-from-motion. In this chapter we will also consider other forms of imaging invariance, such as the invariance of certain shadow features with respect to positions of the light sources that illuminate the scene.

In contrast to previous approaches to line-drawing interpretation, this use of viewpoint invariance requires no restrictive

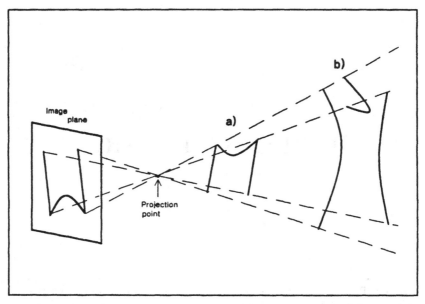

Figure 5-1: The two sets of three-dimensional curves, (a) and (b), project to the identical two-dimensional curves in the image plane. However, reasoning from the image to the scene under the assumption of a camera position that is independent of the objects, we find that the curves at (a) are a much more likely explanation for the image than those at (b). In particular, it is unlikely in this example that separated curve terminations would project to a common point in the image, that a curved line would appear straight, or that non-parallel lines would appear parallel. Therefore, we can infer that the three-space configuration almost certainly satisfies these various constraints, as is the case for the curves shown in (a).

assumptions regarding the scene. The best-known previous approach has been to assume a restricted model of the world and enumerate the possible junction types and other image features that are consistent with the model. This work, as developed by [Huffman, 1971], [Clowes, 1971], [Waltz, 1975], [Mackworth, 1973], [Kanade, 1981], [Sugihara, 1978], and [Draper, 1981], while operating successfully within the specified domain, has proven to be very difficult to extend to general classes of scenes. These models assume that all edges in the image are straight and that the scene consists only of polyhedral objects or polygonal surfaces. Attempts to extend the methodology to scenes with curved lines have had little success. Of even greater practical significance, these methods assume perfect drawings of the scene and do not degrade gracefully in situations with missing and imperfect data.

The use of viewpoint independence assumptions to derive interpretations from various classes of image alignments was first described in [Binford, 1981]. While we have described these inferences in probabilistic terms, Binford pointed out that they are generally reliable enough to be used in a simpler qualitative reasoning scheme, which would only consider the accidental alternatives when faced with contradictory interpretations. In this chapter, we will describe a computer program that uses these inferences in this qualitative way to derive three-space relations from hand-generated image curves. However, a full probabilistic theory and reasoning method would have superior performance in cases where image measurements were less reliable and had a substantial likelihood of being confused with accidental alignments. [Barrow & Tenenbaum, 1981] used another version of the viewpoint independence assumption to infer the three-dimensional shape of individual smooth image curves, a process that would complement the inferences described above. They demonstrated that independence of viewpoint implies that certain interpretations of an image curve are much more likely than others, and that the most likely interpretations correspond to the subjective interpretations of human subjects.

5.1: Three-space inferences from image features

In this section we will enumerate and examine in greater detail the inferences that follow from the assumption of independence of camera position. There are two basic steps involved in the application of each of these inferences: (1) given that an image relation is invariant with respect to a substantial range of viewpoints of a three-space relation, we can expect the image relation to occur often enough to be statistically separable from accidental occurrences and therefore to be a worthwhile objective for a search of the image, and (2) given that we have detected an instance of the relation in an image with sufficient accuracy that it is unlikely to be accidental, we can make the inverse inference that this is an instance of the three-space configuration. A full probabilistic analysis of each inference would require all the steps described in the previous chapter, such as the use of assumptions regarding background distributions and prior probabilities of occurrence for the three-space relations. However, in this chapter we will content ourselves with a qualitative analysis of the invariances and will simply list the conditions under which the image relation could arise through an accident of viewpoint or light-source position. Fortunately, the inferences are reliable enough that they can be used successfully in this type of qualitative reasoning scheme in many common situations.

In addition to inferring three-dimensional structure, the inferences can be used to classify image curves into three distinct classes: those caused by discontinuities in the geometry of an object (edges), in the reflectance of a surface (markings), and in the illumination (shadows). The curves created by discontinuities in object geometry can be further subclassified into those that arise from discontinuities in surface tangent (creases), from surfaces that curve away from the line of sight (limbs), and from structures that are so thin that both opposing edges can only be distinguished as a single image curve (wires). In curves detected from digitized images, there is often local photometric evidence to distinguish among these classes (particularly in the case of wires and shadows [Witkin, 1982]). However, for the sake of generality our discussion will assume that no preliminary classifications have been made, as is the case when interpreting true line drawings. See Figure 5-2 for a table containing pictorial

examples of the image relations that give rise to each of the
following inferences.

1) Collinearity. When any set of three or more distinguish-
able points are collinear in the image, we can infer that they
are also collinear in three-space. The unlikely alternative is that
the points are all coplanar with the position of the camera. This
can be extended to the case of inferring that a straight line in
the image is also a straight line in three-space: the accidental
interpretation is that the line is a planar curve and the camera position happens to lie in the plane containing the curve.
When two straight lines are collinear in the image they must be
collinear in three-space, unless they are coplanar and the camera
is accidentally in the plane containing the lines. This inference
can be used, for example, to bridge gaps in a line caused by
occluding objects or to connect a dashed line.

2) Curvilinearity. The preceding inferences extend to arcs of
constant curvature. In particular, when two curves or four or
more points lie on a circular arc we can assume that they lie on a
common arc in three-space. However, since constant curvature
in three-space does not necessarily project to constant curvature in the image over extended intervals (e.g., circles project to
ellipses), this inference will often only be useful over a limited
local extent.

3) Terminations at a common point. When two or more
curves terminate at a common point in the image—as in the
case of L, Y, K, or higher-order junctions—we can infer that
they terminate at a common point in three-space. The alternative is that there has been an accident in viewpoint in which the
camera happens to lie along a single ray in space connecting the
terminations. In other words, this inference allows us to infer
connectedness in three-space from connectedness in the image
across these junction types, with no special assumptions regarding the scene. This performs one of the most important tasks
of early vision, which is the segmentation of the image into sets

2-D relation	3-D inference	Examples
1. Collinearity of points or line segments	Collinearity in three-space	
2. Curvilinearity of points or arcs	Curvilinearity in three-space	
3. Two or more terminations at a common point	Curves terminate at a common point in three-space	
4. Termination at a continuous curve	Terminating curve is no closer to the camera than the continuous curve	
5. Crossing of continuous curves	Both curves cannot be occluding geometric edges	
6. Parallel curves	Curves are parallel in three-space	
7. Three or more lines converge to a common point	Lines are parallel (seen in perspective) or converge to a common point in three-space	
8. Equal spacing of collinear points or parallel lines	Equal spacing in three-space and parallel lines are coplanar	
9. Relations hold between terminations or virtual lines	Same relation holds between virtual features in three-space	
10. Parallel virtual lines between tangent discontinuities in curves	Curves correspond to geometric edges and their cast shadow boundaries	

Figure 5-2: A summary of the inferences described in the text.

of features that are related in three-space. Accurate segmentation greatly reduces the search space that must be covered when matching world knowledge to the image.

4) Termination at a continuous curve. When an image curve terminates at a continuous curve (a T junction), the terminating curve cannot be closer to the camera than the continuous curve; otherwise, it would be an accident of camera position that the termination happened to occur on the other line. If we have other knowledge regarding the categories of either curve, we can carry information across the junction. The T junction could be the result of three different occurrences: the occlusion of any type of curve by a geometric boundary; the termination of a surface marking, shadow or wire at a geometric boundary; or a combination of surface markings. Therefore, if we know that the terminating curve is a geometric boundary, then we can infer that the continuous curve is also a geometric boundary and we know its direction of occlusion. If we know that the continuous curve is a geometric boundary occluding on the side of the terminating curve, then we can infer that the terminating curve must be a surface marking or shadow. If we know that the terminating curve is a shadow, then we can infer that the continuous curve is a geometric boundary. This last inference is based on the assumption of independence of light-source position, since it would then be an accident if the light source were aligned to cast a shadow that happened to terminate at a surface marking, wire, or shadow cast by another light source.

5) Crossing of continuous curves. When two continuous curves cross one another (an X junction), they cannot both be occluding geometric boundaries. If we know that one curve is an occluding geometric boundary, then the other curve must be closer to the viewer and must be either a wire or the edge of a partially transparent object. If we know that one curve is a shadow, then the other curve must be a surface marking on the same surface, another shadow (cast by a different light source) or a wire that is closer to the viewer than the shadow. Since these cases can often be distinguished on the basis of local evidence during edge detection, shadows provide a powerful source of information regarding the nature of curves across which they fall.

6) Parallelism. We can infer that curves which are parallel in the image are also parallel in three-space. Otherwise, given two non-parallel straight lines the camera must be restrictively placed to create parallelism in the image, and the probability of accidental parallelism greatly decreases as the curves become more complex. The inverse is not always true: parallel lines in three-space may not be parallel in the image due to perspective convergence. However, many instances of parallelism involve separations covering only small visual angles where perspective effects are insignificant—the remaining cases are covered by the following class of inferences.

7) Lines converging to a common point. When three or more lines converge to a common point we can infer that they either converge to a common point in three-space or are parallel in three-space (with the convergence to a vanishing point being an effect of perspective projection). Often there will be a considerable number of parallel lines in a scene (for example, aligned with gravity) that provide a strong basis for making this inference. As a corollary, once a vanishing point is determined, then any line in the image pointing to that vanishing point can be assumed to have a particular orientation in three-space, barring an accident in camera position. [Barnard, 1983] has exploited similar constraints for the interpretation of perspective images.

8) Equal spacing. A series of collinear points or line segments that are equally spaced in three-space will project to collinear points or segments in the image that also have equal spacings—barring perspective effects that lead to a smoothly changing spacing. Therefore, once we have detected collinear elements in the image as described above, we can look for constant or slowly changing spacings in the image that imply constant or near-constant spacings in three-space. For example, this provides information from dotted or dashed lines. It is even more valuable to detect parallel lines with constant spacings in the image, since this implies not only that the lines are parallel in three-space as described above, but also that the lines are coplanar (and equally spaced). Otherwise, it would be an accident that the camera was placed to produce equal spacings between non-coplanar parallel lines.

9) Virtual lines and points. Many of the inferences described above create new distinguished points or lines in the image from combinations of other features. These "virtual" points or lines can be used recursively to generate three-space relations in the same way as the initial features in the image. For example, if we detect a collinearity relationship between a number of points, then these points form a virtual line. If this line is parallel to another line in the image we can infer that the virtual line connecting the points in three-space is parallel to the three-space position of the other line. Virtual features also include the virtual points at the terminations of a curve. For example, when a number of curve terminations are collinear we infer that the terminations are collinear in three-space.

10) Shadows create parallel virtual lines. By combining several of the inferences given above it is possible to create new inferences that apply to the particular case of interpreting illumination discontinuities. When the geometric boundary of some object casts a shadow onto a surface, any tangent discontinuities (corners) in the geometric edges casting the shadow will lead to tangent discontinuities in the cast shadow (unless the light source is accidentally located in the plane of the object tangents). This means that there will be a pairing in the image between tangent breaks in geometric edges and in illumination edges, with the virtual lines formed by these pairs being parallel or converging to a common point.

In perspective imagery there is an *illumination convergence point* in the image through which the images of all illumination rays from a point source pass (this is true even for nearby point sources). If the point source is in front of the camera lens plane, then the convergence point is, of course, the location of the point source in the image. If the light source is behind the camera lens plane, then the illumination convergence point is located at the point of projection of the light source onto the film plane on a ray that passes through the projective center of the camera, and the illumination streams towards this point rather than away from it. If the point source is exactly in the lens plane of the camera, then the perspective effect compensates for divergence from the light source to make the illumination rays parallel in the image.

There are a number of ways to make use of these constraints on illumination. If the illumination convergence point in the image is known for some light source, then any of the virtual lines that are aligned with this convergence point can be inferred to be an instance of a geometric edge casting a shadow. Otherwise it would be an accident of camera position in which unrelated discontinuities happened to align by chance. The matching of geometric edges to shadows not only identifies the class of each image curve, but also provides important information about the three-space separation of the object and surface (proportional to the length of shadow cast for distant sources of illumination). A second application would be to detect illumination convergence points in the image by searching for significant numbers of the virtual lines which are parallel or converge to a common point. Note that all of these inferences remain valid in the presence of multiple sources of illumination.

5.2: Recovery of 3D properties from line drawings

The application of the inferences given in the previous section to actual images requires methods for combining information from the different constraints and for resolving conflicting interpretations. The inferences then result in the categorization of image curves and the specification of three-space relations between features of the image. Many of the inferences are built on the results of previous inferences that must be combined and propagated to adjacent structures as they occur. For our program, we have chosen to use a straightforward form of constraint propagation, in which the results of previous inferences are systematically explored. For example, when an image curve is categorized as a shadow or geometric boundary, this leads to a systematic examination of all junctions between that curve and adjacent curves to see whether inferences can be propagated across the junctions. An important issue is the resolution of inconsistencies in the constraint network—for example, inferences that assign two different categorizations to the same curve. Although the possibility of incorrect inferences would be vanishingly small given perfectly accurate image measurements, in practice there will be some probability of errors given the limitations of accuracy in image measurements. A reasonable strategy, which we have adopted in our system, is to ignore both alternatives of a conflicting interpretation unless one has more sources of evidence behind it than the other, in which case it is chosen as the correct interpretation.

Although it is common for many interpretations to be over-constrained—with multiple inferences lending support to the same conclusion—it is also common for some aspects of the final result to be unspecified. The purpose of these inferences should not be viewed as the construction of a complete depth map or "intrinsic image." What they provide is a partial segmentation of the image into sets of related features as well as constraints on three-space relations between components of the scene. This information can still greatly reduce the search space that must be explored in comparing the image to specific models, as described in Chapter 7. It can also be used in combination with information from whatever other sources of information are available, such as shading or stereo.

The sequential style of constraint propagation is used in the computer program described in the next section. However, a parallel model for the application of the inferences would be more in keeping with our knowledge of the human visual system. This parallel model would be based on perceptual operations of the type described in the previous chapter, which would be applied uniformly to the entire image and would detect all instances of significant collinearity, parallelism, convergence, endpoint proximity (junctions), etc., with inferences being propagated in parallel between neighboring features. The most complete use of these inferences would be obtained by making explicit estimates of the probability that each feature could be accidental. These estimates would be based upon the accuracy with which each relation can be measured in the image and on the probability that an accidental camera position or other accident might have occured to the measured degree of precision. These probability estimates could be used to resolve inconsistencies in a more accurate way and to focus attention of later stages of the visual process on the more certain pieces of information. In addition, they would allow the inferences described here to be integrated with other types of inference based on probabilistic properties of the world. An example is the perceptual detection of skewed symmetry explored by [Kanade, 1981], which is based on the assumption that bilateral symmetry is common in the world rather than on the assumption of independence of viewpoint. However, valuable as the probabilistic reasoning might be, it should also be emphasized that in typical scenes there are many inferences that can be made with great certainty, and many scenes are sufficiently overconstrained to make the problem of incorrect inferences one of secondary importance. The following section describes a computer program based upon these simpler assumptions.

5.3: A demonstration of three-space inference

We have implemented a computer program that applies many of the inferences described above to hand-input image curves. The program is written in MACLISP and runs on a DEC KL-10 computer. This program uses a simple form of constraint propagation, in which all the inferences resulting from any categorization or relation are systematically propagated until there are no further changes (in practice, this process seldom proceeds through more than one or two levels of inference). The image relations are detected by testing image features against preset thresholds (e.g., lines are considered parallel if they are within 10 degrees in orientation and are closer in proximity than the length of the shortest line). The success of these simple criteria for detecting image relations depends upon the high quality of the hand-traced image curves. This is particularly true for detecting curve terminations and junctions, which are often missed or poorly located by current edge detection methods. However, there is reason to believe that substantially improved techniques for locating terminations and forming junctions can be developed in the future [Binford, 1981].

The curves input to the program are represented as cubic splines. Junctions are formed after input based on proximity of terminations to other terminations or curves, using a preset threshold for judging proximity. Figure 5-3(a) shows the cubic spline input data that was traced by hand from an aerial photograph taken over San Francisco airport. The program was also given the direction and angle of illumination, although as was previously described this information could probably be derived directly from the image.

Figure 5-3(b) shows dotted lines parallel to the projected direction of illumination which connect pairs of tangent discontinuities (the use of these shadow features was described in part 10 of the list of inferences above). From these, the pro-

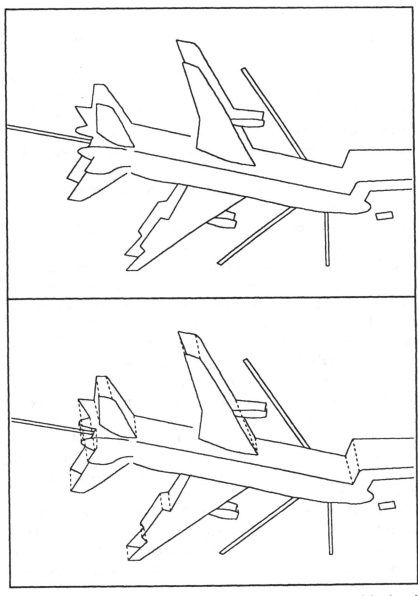

Figure 5-3(a,b): The curves shown at the top were traced by hand from an aerial photograph of an airplane at San Francisco airport. Figure (b) shows the detection of pairs of tangent discontinuities parallel to the known direction of illumination, which are then used to infer curve categorizations and shadow matches.

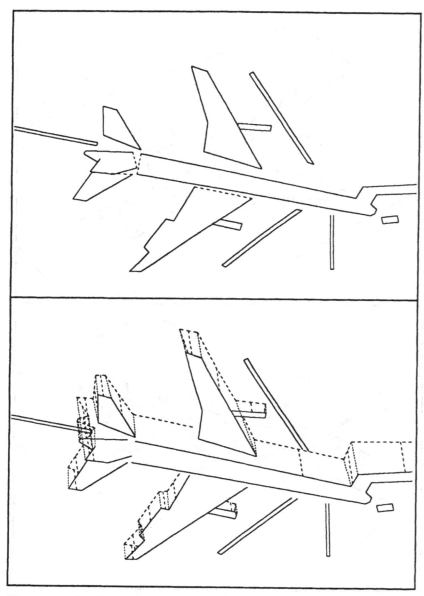

Figure 5-3(c,d): Figure (c) shows the geometric surface segmentation that results from curve categorization and region formation. Figure (d) shows shadow curves as dotted lines connected to the geometric edges that are presumed to have cast them.

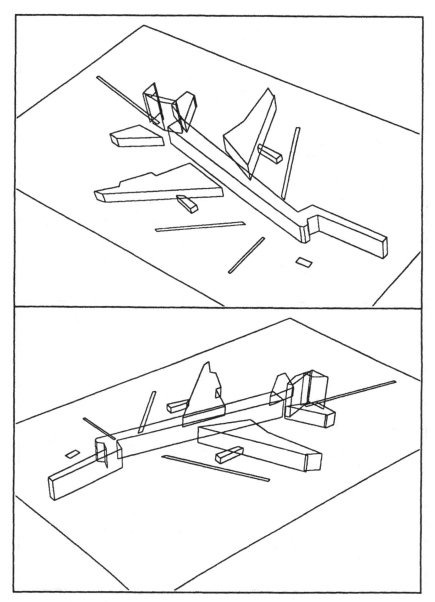

Figure 5-3(e,f): These figures show the final three-dimensional description that was computed for this data. It shows the height of segmented surfaces above a ground plane. Since the result is three-dimensional, it can be viewed from any position.

gram categorizes the curves in the pairings as geometric edges or shadow boundaries, depending upon which end they occupy of each pair. These constraints on curve categories are propagated through neighboring junctions, using the inferences described in part 4 of the list above. The program then attempts to form a closed geometric boundary around individual regions, using the previous categorizations of certain curves as geometric boundaries. Each curve is followed through all unambiguous continuations (collinear segments or curves that terminate at the same location), in an attempt to form closed regions. A region is accepted if a curve and its unambiguous continuations form at least 75% of the perimeter of the region. Another source of evidence used to form region segmentations is parallelism between geometric boundaries, which is accepted when two geometric boundaries are parallel to within 10 degrees and also form 75% of the boundary of some region. The result of these geometric surface segmentation processes is shown in Figure 5-3(c).

Figure 5-3(d) shows shadow boundaries represented as dotted lines, and pairings are given between geometric boundaries and the shadows that they cast. From this information, it is possible to calculate the relative separations of surfaces based upon the lengths of the shadows that they cast onto other surfaces. Given a distant point source with parallel illumination rays, the length of a cast shadow is proportional to the separation of the geometric boundary and shadow curve. If the orientation of the shadowed surface is known, then the orientation of the geometric edge casting the shadow can be determined. The program initially assumes that surfaces are parallel to the camera plane and then looks for evidence to the contrary, based upon relative separations at different locations along a geometric boundary and its cast shadow. For example, the tail surface of the airplane is found to be approximately vertical with respect to the ground. See [Shafer, 1982] for a much more detailed analysis of the use of shadow matches for constraining orientation.

From this set of surface segmentations, orientations and separations, it is possible to construct a partial three-dimensional geometric description of the scene as shown in Figure 5-3(e). This representation assumes that surfaces are horizontal in the absence of other evidence, and shows each surface as a solid box extending down to a uniform ground plane. Since this is a three-dimensional representation it can be rotated and viewed from other angles as shown in Figure 5-3(f).

As mentioned earlier, it is not possible in general to construct a full depth map of the image and this should not be considered the major purpose of the inferences. Aerial photography has lighting conditions that are particularly suited to generating fairly complete depth descriptions. The assumptions regarding horizontal surfaces would not be as reasonable for many other types of images. However, even in the absence of any information from shadows and without being able to determine surface orientations, the many other inferences allow segmentation of the image and the inference of many types of three-space relations. In fact, for the purposes of recognition, it can be argued that segmentation and symbolic relations do more to reduce the search space for matching than does a simple depth map of the scene. The purpose of this program is to illustrate the strength and generality of these inferences derived from viewpoint invariance. Clearly, much more work would be required to develop a program that did not have the arbitrary detection thresholds and that could operate successfully with real image data.

5.4: Conclusions and future development

In this chapter, we have described and demonstrated a number of inferences for the interpretation of image curves that do not require restrictive assumptions about the nature of the scene. The inferences are based on the simple assumptions that the camera viewpoint and light-source positions are independent of the objects in the scene—assumptions that are valid for most classes of images. In cases where these assumptions are violated—as in some engineering drawings—human vision has difficulty in providing three-dimensional interpretations. These inferences can be applied on their own to segment and provide three-space inferences from the image, as was demonstrated in the computer program. However, an important remaining challenge is to integrate this form of inference with the full set of perceptual operations described in the other chapters of this book. This would require a detailed statistical analysis of each type of inference, and would require inference methods that could combine and use these statistical results. Aspects of this problem will be described in Chapter 6, but much research remains to be done before final answers can be given.

There are also ways in which the simple, qualitative application of these inferences could be improved. One obvious need is for better methods for detecting and locating curve terminations and junctions in digitized images, since these provide a basic and reliable source of information. It is also important to accurately localize the curves themselves, as well as tangent discontinuities. Another significant goal would be to combine the information from these inferences with other sources of three-dimensional information, such as that produced by the interpretation of stereo, motion, or shading. The simple depth-map representation is inadequate for representing many of the constraints produced by the three-space inferences described in this chapter, so more complex forms for representing three-space constraints would need to be developed.

Chapter 6

MODEL-BASED SEARCH AND INFERENCE

ONE of the central topics of artificial intelligence research has been the problem of efficient search. For many problems in AI, there are straightforward methods for solving a problem by enumerating over a large set of possible interpretations and looking for those that are consistent with the given data. Unfortunately, in many cases the set of possible interpretations is combinatorially large and cannot be enumerated in a reasonable amount of time. Therefore, a substantial amount of AI research has been devoted to finding methods for speeding up the search process. These methods fall into two classes: the so-called weak methods that look for general purpose algorithms that could be applied to any search problem, and the strong methods that attempt to apply specific knowledge of the problem at hand. Recent AI research has tended to concentrate on the strong methods—in particular, making use of large amounts of world knowledge that can often be applied to find a quick path through what would otherwise be an intractable search space.

The problem of model-based computer vision falls neatly into this category of search problems. As will be demonstrated in the next chapter, it is usually possible to determine reliably the correctness of some model-based interpretation of an image once a match has been suggested. It is also straightforward to enumerate all possible interpretations for an image. The significant remaining problem is reducing the size of this search space. As in other areas of AI, there is no single, magical method for solving this problem—it is necessary to incorporate many types of world knowledge and many intermediate problem representations to achieve substantial success. Even then, the performance of any system, including human vision, will be inadequate for some subset of the possible tasks. The previous chapters have been concerned with the use of perceptual organization to provide information which reduces the range of possible interpretations that must be considered for a collection of image features. This chapter will examine methods for the actual enumeration of this search space and describe the ways in which perceptual organization can have a major impact.

There are two major components of the search space that must be covered during image interpretation. The first component deals with the space of possible viewpoints on each object. Since spatial information in the image is highly dependent upon viewpoint, any strong predictions for spatial appearance of an object are likely to apply to only a relatively small subrange of the possible viewpoints. Therefore, a complete search must enumerate over the various discrete ranges of viewpoints that need to be considered. The seemingly large size of this search space has been a major factor leading researchers to avoid searching over the range of viewpoints and instead direct their efforts into the derivation of three-dimensional structure from the image. While it is true that direct three-dimensional information would reduce the complexity of this component, it is also the case that general purpose vision requires recognition even in the absence of bottom-up depth information. Fortunately, as will be described in the following section, the size and complexity of this search space turns out to be quite manageable, particularly if we make use of perceptual groupings.

The second major component of the search space is the problem of selecting an object description for matching from among the potentially vast number of objects that could appear in a given scene. In the absence of well-established methods for recognizing even single, known objects, this problem has not been a major focus of research. However, this component of the search problem is potentially much larger than the space of possible viewpoints, and we can expect it to increase in importance with each improvement in the performance of computer vision systems. Perceptual organization can again play a major role in reducing the size of this search. We will describe an inference procedure—borrowed from recent work on expert systems—for using the various groupings that are detected in an image to update our expectations regarding the presence of particular objects. These changed expectations can result in very large reductions in the amount of search required for recognition. Additionally, these methods allow us to combine information from many different sources into a single estimate of whether some object is present. For example, we can make use of contextual information in which the recognition of one object in a scene leads us to increased expectations for certain other objects. This can also be combined with color, texture, motion, and information from other sensory modalities. These methods are of interest from the psychological viewpoint as well as for their application to computer vision.

6.1: Searching the space of possible viewpoints

The space of possible viewpoints may at first seem to be too large for carrying out an exhaustive, quantitative search over all the possible projections of an object into an image. There are a total of six viewpoint parameters for a camera of known focal length, which specify an object's location in the image, distance from the camera, and orientation in three-space. However, if we only predict the relative locations of features in the image, these predictions will be invariant with respect to location in the image and rotation in the image plane—leaving only a three-parameter space determining distance from the camera and rotation out of the image plane. Of greater significance is the fact that relations between object features usually vary slowly and smoothly with respect to changes in viewpoint. Although there are discontinuities in some relations from certain viewpoints, there is no need to include every possible prediction, so these discontinuous cases can be ignored. This means that it is unnecessary to sample the parameter ranges very densely. For a fairly wide range in each parameter, it is possible to make quantitative predictions regarding relative locations of features in the image that are adequately bounded for avoiding a profusion of false matches.

A straightforward—but very highly-optimized—application of this search over the space of viewpoint parameters is described by [Goad, 1983]. His model-based vision system searches for sets of edges in an image which could be the consistent projection of three-dimensional edges of a known object. The method consists of a depth-first search procedure that considers discrete sets of ranges of viewpoint parameters at each node in the search tree. This search cycles repeatedly through three steps as it descends through each level of the search. These steps can be referred to as *predict, match,* and *back-project.* The first step predicts the orientation, location, length, and curvature of some edge in the image, with the orientation and location being relative to any already-matched features. If no features have been matched yet, then the prediction may not be restricted to any particular location or orientation, and will therefore match any edge in the image of the correct length or curvature. The second step consists of searching the image for all features which match the given prediction. For each of these matches, a new child node is created in the search tree for further search. The third step of back-projection operates at each new node of the tree to use the measured location of a matched image feature to narrow the ranges under consideration for the viewpoint parameters. It is this back-projection step which gives the sequential search procedure its strong advantage over methods which attempt to predict the appearance of a complete image which is then matched as a whole. For well specified models, only about three image features need to be matched before the viewpoint is constrained to approximately a single position. Thereafter, further levels of the search are unlikely to find false matches in the image and so there is no further expansion of the search tree. Since image features may be missing due to the unreliability of feature detectors and the presence of occlusion, it is necessary to expand the search space somewhat to allow for missing features. Therefore, each node of the search tree may sometimes also be skipped and matching will proceed to the next level without a match and without further restriction on the viewpoint range.

The back-projection step is the most difficult from a mathematical viewpoint, since there are no simple, closed-form solutions for determining the range of viewpoint parameters consistent with a given set of image matches. Goad cleverly handles this problem and also achieves large gains in speed by making use of an extensive precomputation system. During the precomputation phase, values which will be needed at runtime for various stages of the search are precomputed and stored in tables at an appropriate level of resolution. The result is that typical objects can be robustly recognized in a viewpoint-independent manner in times on the order of one second while the system is running on a MC68000 microprocessor. This is a powerful demonstration of the fact that searches over the range of possible viewpoints can be accomplished with modest amounts of computation.

In addition to searching through the space of parameters determining viewpoint, it is possible to also include parameters of variation in a model arising from generic object descriptions. This problem was a major focus of the ACRONYM system [Brooks, 1981], which was also one of the first model-based vision systems to implement the predict, match, back-project cycle. ACRONYM had more general goals than Goad's system, in that it included this problem of searching over a space of model parameters and then solving for the resulting bounds on image measurements using a general symbolic algebra system. ACRONYM was able to integrate knowledge from many different sources with this symbolic constraint system, including prior restrictions on viewpoint and depth information from stereo correspondence or other sources. Unfortunately, the symbolic equation solver was unable to solve for precise bounds from the trigonometric equations describing projection from arbitrary viewpoints, so the capability of the system for quantitatively searching the space of possible viewpoints in two-dimensional image data was quite limited. However, it is one of the most comprehensive vision systems to date that has been based on a systematic search for spatial correspondence.

A similar search process has recently been used by [Grimson & Lozano-Pérez, 1983] to recognize objects from sparse range data or the output of tactile sensors. They examine and analyze a number of local position-independent constraints on pairs of features that can be used to prune the search space. However, their methods require the use of range and surface orientation data and do not extend to the use of two-dimensional features that are being considered here.

One open problem in applying the above methods for searching the space of viewpoints is how to choose the optimal subdivision of the viewpoint parameters into discrete ranges. There is a tradeoff between choosing small ranges of parameters, which would require more discrete cases to be considered, and choosing larger ranges, in which case there may be poorer discrimination in image measurements leading to more false matches. In practice it appears that choosing fixed, moderately-large ranges works well, but this will certainly not always be the optimal choice.

6.1.1: The role of perceptual organization

Perceptual groupings can play two important roles in reducing the size of this search space over viewpoints and object parameters. First, they can greatly reduce the number of false matches that must be considered at a given stage of the search. For example, if we are searching for sets of parallel edges, it is likely that there will be far fewer candidates to consider than the number of all edges in the image. As the perceptual groupings become more complex, the probability of finding false matches decreases even further. In quantitative terms, if the average density of features being matched decreases from D to D', then the branching factor at each level of the search tree will be reduced by a factor of D'/D (assuming uniform distribution of features).

Secondly, perceptual groupings can lead to much stronger results during the back-projection step than isolated features. For example, matching a single edge to a model puts far fewer constraints upon viewpoint than would a match to a grouping of several edges. Since it is the unconstrained viewpoint during the first few levels of the search tree that accounts for most of the size of the search space, the ability to strongly constrain viewpoint from the initial match can result in a dramatic reduction in search. A similar point was noted in [Brooks, 1982] for the solution of back-constraints in the ACRONYM system.

Balanced against the advantages of using perceptual groupings are the costs of performing perceptual organization. However, although these costs may be substantial, the grouping only needs to be performed once for all objects and therefore its cost for each attempted match will not be significant if enough objects are being considered. Another requirement for making use of perceptual groupings is that the object's projection must contain perceptually significant groupings often enough to make them worth searching for. This requirement seems to be met for almost all objects. However, as was shown by the example of Figure 1-4 (in the case in which a person is told that the image contains a bicycle) human vision seems to be fully capable of searching the set of possible viewpoints for a known object even when there are no significant groupings beyond the level of edges.

The ACRONYM vision system performed its matching against a particular form of image groupings known as ribbons. Although these were not detected strictly bottom-up—some parameters of the ribbons were specified top-down from knowledge of a particular object—the ribbons themselves were a combination of several of the types of perceptual groupings that we have discussed in previous chapters. A ribbon was defined as an elongated shape in the image that was the projection of a generalized cylinder [Binford, 1971]. The detection of the ribbons was performed by a search procedure among straight edge segments, which looked for a combination of endpoint proximity, collinearity, parallelism of opposing sides and a certain overall degree of closure for the region. Given the poor quality of the initial edge data, this algorithm did a reasonable job of selecting perceptually significant structures for use by the matching algorithm.

6.2: Searching the space of possible objects

In comparison with the space of possible viewpoints, which is of fairly constant size for each object, the space of all possible objects is much larger and more open-ended. The search over viewpoints consists of a small number of discrete cases—within which continuous quantitative search techniques are used—whereas the space of all possible objects seems to contain very large numbers of discrete cases. While there is some overlap between the two problems, we will be making use of a different method to handle the problem of searching among the set of possible objects. The most important aspect of this search problem seems to be the capability to combine information from many different sources to determine our expectations for the presence of a particular object. For example, we will want to make use of the simultaneous presence of a number of different perceptual groupings, texture measures, color, size, contextual information and any available prior knowledge. None of this information is likely to be absolute in the sense that it always indicates the presence of a certain object or is always present when the object is present. Therefore, in order to make maximum use of this information we will use a probabilistic method which can represent the relative importance of the various factors.

Fortunately, there has been a considerable amount of recent work in the development of methods for combining probabilistic expectations, much of it motivated by the need to solve this problem for use in diagnostic expert systems. We will first outline a general model of search which can make use of probabilistic information to choose the optimal search path, and will then apply some of the recent work on the combination of probabilistic evidence to the problem of visual recognition. Finally, we will examine the integration of this approach with hierarchical object descriptions and other components of a vision system.

6.2.1: A model of probabilistic search

If we had an infinitely large parallel computer, it would be possible to search simultaneously for every known object, so the length of time required for recognition would be independent of the number of alternatives under consideration. However, even for such a highly parallel system as the human brain, recognition is much easier if there are prior expectations for the presence of a particular object (as is shown by the examples in Figures 1-4 and 1-5). The methods we will be using assume serial search through a sequence of objects, but would extend in the obvious way if a limited amount of parallelism were available to search for some fixed number of possibilities simultaneously. The objective will be to order the search in such a way as to reduce the total amount of computation required for recognition, and to update this ordering as new evidence is brought to bear.

Let P_k be the probability that object k is present in the image. Let W_k be the amount of work (i.e., computation time) required to verify the presence of object k by performing the subsequent search over the range of viewpoints and model parameters. Then we can define a measure R_k which will be used to determine the object ranking:

$$R_k = \frac{W_k}{P_k}$$

Given this measure, the optimal ranking of objects during search will be in terms of increasing values of R_k:

$$(R_1, R_2, R_3, ...R_n), \quad R_i \le R_{i+1}$$

In other words, our effort will have the highest payoff if we are searching for the object that requires the least amount of work on average for a successful detection. The inclusion of the W_k terms avoids some semantic difficulties in what is defined to be an object, since if two separate objects of the same ranking are combined and named to be a single object, both their P_k and W_k terms will add together and there will be no change in the resulting ranking.

In order to calculate the average search time, we can sum up the amount of work expended in trying to recognize each object times the probability that that particular position in the ranking will be reached:

$$A = W_1 + W_2(1 - P_1) + W_3(1 - P_1)(1 - P_2) + \cdots + W_n \prod_{j=1}^{n-1}(1 - P_j)$$

$$= \sum_{i=1}^{n} W_i \prod_{j=1}^{i-1}(1 - P_j).$$

It is always possible that no objects will be recognized in some images, but this just means that the probabilities will not sum to 1 and does not affect the above formulas. We can also calculate the median search time, which is equal to the sum of all the W_k terms up to the point at which the P_k terms add up to 0.5. Of course, an image is likely to contain many objects, and we have only been calculating the time required to recognize the first object. However, as soon as one object is recognized it provides contextual information which updates the rankings and aids in the search process, so it would be improper to incorporate multiple object recognition in a single ranking as given above.

Our objective will be to use all available evidence to update the rankings of objects so as to minimize the average recognition times. Assuming that the W_k terms are fixed, our objective will be to increase the P_k probability terms by making use of evidence regarding the particular image under consideration. As shown in the formula above for average recognition times, any increase in a P_k has an effect on the product term for all objects which occur lower in the ranking. There is a further positive effect due to any changes in the ranking caused by the updated value.

6.2.2: Evidential reasoning for reducing search

Methods for combining information from different sources of evidence to update probabilistic expectations have received a considerable amount of attention recently for use in medical expert systems. In many respects, the problem of diagnosing a disease from a number of symptoms is very similar to the problem of trying to identify an object from a number of different sources of evidence in the image. However, the image recognition problem as we have framed it is actually simpler, since we will be using evidential reasoning only to speed up the search process across different objects rather than to make the final judgment of correctness for a match. The final decision regarding the correctness of a match can rely on much more reliable quantitative matching as described in the next chapter. Therefore, some of the more complex aspects of recent work on evidential reasoning in medicine are unlikely to be needed or useful. For example, there has been a considerable amount of interest recently in the Dempster-Shafer model of evidential reasoning which allows the user to represent degrees of ignorance as well as expected probabilities [Shafer, 1976; Lowrance & Garvey, 1982]. However, there seems to be no need for an estimate of ignorance when calculating rankings for a search process, so the many complications in applying this type of method need not concern us.

The problem of decision-making under uncertainty has been a longstanding topic of research in mathematics, based on the use of conditional probabilities and Bayesian statistics. However, the use of Bayesian statistics was rejected by the initial researchers in medical expert systems, since they assumed that it would either require unrealistic independence assumptions or an impossibly large number of known statistical parameters. Instead, they developed various heuristic methods for combining evidence which seemingly eased these requirements [Shortliffe & Buchanan, 1975; Szolovitz & Pauker, 1978]. However, Charniak has shown in an interesting recent paper, [Charniak, 1983], that these heuristic methods actually correspond to Bayesian reasoning under certain reasonable assumptions and that they can be formalized within the framework of conditional probabilities. These methods can be readily applied to many situations requiring evidential reasoning. The rest of this section presents an overview of Charniak's techniques and describes how they can be applied to the problem of model-based vision.

Let us assume that we have detected a number of features or properties of the image, $f_1, \ldots, f_n$, and wish to estimate the probability of the presence of a particular object model, m_i. In terms of conditional probabilities, this means that we want to calculate $P(m_i|f_1, \ldots, f_n)$. It would obviously be impossible to store the value of this quantity for all possible combinations of features, which is why we need methods for combining evidence.

Charniak bases his method on the following form of Bayes's theorem:

$$P(m_i|f_1,\ldots,f_n) = \frac{P(m_i) * P(f_1,\ldots,f_n|m_i)}{P(f_1,\ldots,f_n)}$$

In order to express this formula as a combination of probabilities for the individual features, we must make two independence assumptions:

$$P(f_i\&f_j) = P(f_i) * P(f_j)$$

$$P(f_i\&f_j|m) = P(f_i|m) * P(f_j|m)$$

There will be many cases in which each of these independence assumptions are violated, but these cases can be handled by methods which will be described below. The independence assumptions allow us to break the joint probabilities into combinations of individual terms:

$$P(m_i|f_1,\ldots,f_n) = \frac{P(m_i) * P(f_1|m_i) * \cdots * P(f_n|m_i)}{P(f_1) * \cdots * P(f_n)}$$

$$= P(m_i) * \left[\frac{P(f_1|m_i)}{P(f_1)}\right] * \cdots * \left[\frac{P(f_n|m_i)}{P(f_n)}\right]$$

This last formula gives the updating term for each new f_j. We start with some initial probability estimate $P(m_i)$ for an object, and for each new feature which is detected we multiply this estimate by $\frac{P(f_j|m_i)}{P(f_j)}$.

This still leaves the problem of what to do when the independence assumptions we made above are violated. The first assumption, $P(f_i\&f_j) = P(f_i) * P(f_j)$, is very restrictive. In fact, it is in contradiction to the whole enterprise in which we are engaged, since it will be violated whenever two features tend to arise together from the presence of a single object. However, Charniak points out that this assumption is used only to determine the denominator of the above conditional expression, and is independent of any particular object. Therefore, any violations of this assumption will affect all object probability estimates by the same factor, and will have no effect upon probability rankings. This explains why it is possible to keep multiplying a probability by new factors which may cause its value to become greater than 1. The final result should therefore not be interpreted as an absolute probability estimate, but should be used only for establishing relative rankings. Happily, this is all that is needed for our application of ordering the search process.

The one remaining problem is the second independence assumption, $P(f_i \& f_j | m) = P(f_i | m) * P(f_j | m)$, which states that two features are independent given the presence of a particular object. This assumption will be violated if what we are calling a single object actually has different subcases, one of which tends to contain the features while the other one doesn't. Charniak's solution in this case would be to introduce states which represent the different subcases and to express the conditional probabilities with respect to these subcases. There may be other situations in which the independence of features given an object does not hold, but it is always possible to just explicitly remember the joint probability of $P(f_i \& f_j | m)$ in these cases, and to plug this value into our updating formula whenever the two features are both present. Therefore, we are assuming independence as our default assumption, but are also retaining the option to include any information regarding non-independence.

6.2.3: Evidential reasoning in vision

The attractive feature of using evidential reasoning for computer vision is that it allows us to combine information of varying reliability from many sources, even though no particular item of evidence is necessary or sufficient for recognizing a particular object. For example, if we have just walked into an office (or have already recognized one object in an image which suggests that we are looking at an office environment), we would like to increase our expectations of seeing certain other objects, such as desks, chairs, filing cabinets, telephones, etc., but we don't want to completely rule out the surprising presence of any other objects. Given that a desk is only one of thousands of common objects with which we interact, our initial P(desk) in any scene might be only 0.001. However, since we often expect to be in an office when we see a desk, say P(office|desk) = 0.5, and since our initial estimate for the presence of a desk was based on a low probability for being in an office, P(office) = 0.01, we can now update our P(desk) by a factor of 0.5/0.01 = 50. As Charniak points out, we could just remember this updating factor rather than the separate probabilities. Therefore, P(desk) now equals 0.05 (for any given part of the scene), which will move it much closer towards the front in our rankings of objects to consider. If we now consider some perceptual grouping of a number of equally spaced horizontal lines which could be caused by the drawers of a desk, we can increase our expectation for a desk at that location by another substantial factor. If the region between these lines is of a color that is statistically associated with desks, or if it has a wood-grain texture, we can multiply these factors into our expectations. In this way, we can quickly move this object to the head of the ranked list, even though none of the items of evidence is in itself very conclusive.

One obvious concern is that we need to avoid spending so much time on this updating and ranking task that we undo the savings we are trying to make in the search process. It would clearly be impractical to update our expectations for every known object for every item of evidence that we encounter. The solution is to adopt some threshold on the significance of object probabilities which limits the number of objects that will be updated. We should only consider those objects for which we have either a high current expectation or for which the evidence under consideration carries a strong implication. This will fail to uncover those objects which could achieve a strong significance after combining many individual items of evidence, none of which are even moderately strong. However, it is not clear that even human vision would perform well in these situations.

Another problem is that the Bayesian scheme assumes that all evidence is being collected for a single conclusion. In medical diagnosis, this is known as the multiple disease problem, since a set of symptoms may be the result of more than one disease. Fortunately, the consequences of violating this assumption are not very severe. In the medical situation, it is common to just assume that all evidence is referring to a single disease, and then to use some other method of looking at the top few highest-ranked conclusions to see which combinations of them best explain the evidence. Since in computer vision we will already be relying on other methods to verify our final interpretations, this problem should be of limited consequence. On the other hand, a typical image will contain a substantial number of different objects, so it would be useful to make some effort to see that the evidence we are combining refers to a single object. Contextual information will typically update our expectations for an entire scene, but perceptual groupings, color, or texture refer only to a particular region. Therefore, we should only combine these items of evidence if they are related by enclosure, connectedness, adjacency, or other indication that they are related in the image. Even better, we could weight their combination by the degree to which these criteria are met.

Many readers may be wondering at this point exactly what the dividing line is between an object and a feature. After all, an object can be built up from a hierarchy of component parts, each of which can be recognized in its own right. For example, we can recognize the shape of the human body as a whole, or recognition can proceed by first recognizing an eye or a hand and proceeding from that to recognizing other components. So, should our ranked list of objects consist of overall object descriptions or merely the simplest level of components out of which complex objects can be assembled? The answer is clearly that both should be included, and that each type of description will be useful in different types of images. A desk is part of an office in much the same way that a handle is part of a desk. We can proceed from the whole to the part or from the part to the whole depending upon which is easier to recognize first. We can make use of either evidential reasoning or of explicit model parameters as described in the previous section to propagate information in either direction. The obvious result is that our list of possible objects is going to be large, which makes the use of evidential reasoning all the more important.

We have been assuming that the various probability values are somehow known in advance. One important extension would be to have these acquired by a learning system and continuously updated as the system gains visual experience. Since the purpose of these values is to speed up system performance, the system would still function given rough initial values for new objects, but would gradually gain in speed as the values became more and more accurate. It would be straightforward to update the values of $P(f_j)$ and $P(f_j|m_i)$ for the features after each successful recognition has occurred. The more difficult problem would be to recognize instances in which the independence assumptions do not hold, and to introduce intermediate states or the $P(f_i \& f_j|m)$ values for combinations of features. This is related to the problem of inferring optimal object categorizations from a sample of data and is clearly a topic needing further research. However, even without recognizing violations of independence, the automatic updating of the conditional probabilities would greatly simplify the input of information.

6.3: Summary

Methods for searching over the range of possible viewpoints and parameterized instances of an object are now fairly well understood, at least for well-structured objects. They have been successfully implemented in working systems, and constitute an existence proof for the fact that bottom-up extraction of depth information is not necessary for recognizing three-dimensional objects. As new capabilities are introduced for performing perceptual organization, they can be expected to result in dramatic improvements in speed over the exhaustive consideration of every edge or other primitive feature in an image. The SCERPO vision system described in Chapter 8 demonstrates some of these capabilities.

The topic of the second section of this chapter, the use of evidential reasoning, is more speculative in nature, but it could eventually prove to be even more important since it deals with an inherently larger search space. Although there are many aspects that could benefit from further research, enough has been developed so that it should be of practical use in, say, an industrial vision system recognizing a large number of known objects. These methods are interesting from the psychological viewpoint because they allow a system to incorporate many different sources of evidence that are probabilistic in nature, including contextual expectations. Human vision seems to make extensive use of contextual information from both cognitive and strictly visual sources (see [Biederman, 1981] for many relevant experiments). Another potential impact of evidential reasoning is that the ability to combine information from different sources could help to reduce some of the isolation among various subfields of computer vision. For example, it could encourage the use of color, which is not sufficient in itself for solving most visual problems but can be very useful in conjunction with other information. Finally, the potential for building a system which learns to improve its performance as it gains visual experience is of obvious long-term interest.

Chapter 7

THE VERIFICATION
OF IMAGE
INTERPRETATIONS

ONE OF the central arguments for the importance of perceptual organization is that it reduces the otherwise enormous task of searching for spatial correspondence between image features and prior knowledge of objects. However, this argument is based on the assumption that the final verification of the correctness of a set of correspondences can be carried out quickly and reliably as part of the search process. In this chapter, some practical methods will be described for performing this verification process, in particular for determining the viewpoint and unknown parameters of a three-dimensional object as accurately as possible and measuring the degree to which the spatial information in the image agrees with the predictions of the model.

It may seem that this use of spatial information for verification places too much emphasis on a single aspect of correspondence while ignoring shading, color, texture, context, and other dimensions along which comparisons could be made between image and model. However, there is good reason to believe that spatial information is the dominant source of information for verification in most recognition tasks, as well as being a prerequisite to the application of the other measures. If we compare the number and accuracy of spatial predictions which can be made for a typical object with the number and accuracy of predictions for the other classes of features, the sheer quantity of spatial information seems to be much greater for most object classes. This can be intuitively demonstrated by comparing a line drawing, in which much of the spatial information is present and the other dimensions are missing, with an image containing only patches of shading, color or texture with loosely defined boundaries. The certainty we would ascribe to an interpretation is likely to be far stronger in the first case than in the second. There are some classes of objects (for example, some types of natural vegetation) which may be defined more by color and texture than by shape, but these cases seem to be in a distinct minority. Even in these cases, it is usually necessary to first establish a tentative shape correspondence between image and object before the other dimensions can be accurately compared for specific regions of the object.

The most difficult aspect of using spatial information is that it is highly dependent upon viewpoint and shape variations of the object. The search methods outlined in the previous chapter establish tentative correspondences between some selected object features and image features. These search methods discretize the ranges of variation, and invariably discard some degree of spatial accuracy for the sake of efficiency of the representation. In order to verify these interpretations, it is necessary to apply a second level of analysis to these initial correspondences to determine values for the viewpoint and shape parameters which are accurate to the limits of the data. By looking for consistency among these correspondences and by using the calculated parameters to predict further matches at specific locations, it is possible to carry out the verification with great reliability for most types of objects. Currently, almost no vi-

sion systems have mechanisms which make use of image locations in this way to their full accuracy. This is no doubt due to
the difficulty of the mathematical problem of determining exact
viewpoint from initial matches. This chapter will be principally
devoted to developing a practical and efficient solution to this
mathematical problem.

7.1: Viewpoint determination in human vision

The extent to which human vision makes use of spatial information during recognition has not been the object of much study
within the field of psychology. However, it is clear that accurate determination of object location, orientation, and internal
parameters is necessary for many visual and motor tasks, such
as the task of judging a three-dimensional length from a two-
dimensional image. It also seems clear that human vision makes
full use of accurate viewpoint estimates to judge the consistency
and plausibility of an interpretation. Any amateur artist knows
that it is essential to get the "proportions" correct in order to
produce a realistic drawing of an object. Many computer vision
systems which look only at connectivity patterns or qualitative
shape descriptions throw out much of this important spatial information. While viewpoint-invariant properties are important
for reducing the search space leading to recognition, the process
of verifying an interpretation has much to gain from being based
upon as accurate a determination of viewpoint as possible.

One interesting and relevant piece of psychological data on
viewpoint determination is the work on mental rotation [Shep-
ard & Metzler, 1971; Cooper & Shepard, 1984]. In this experiment, subjects were asked to compare two perspective line
drawings of simple objects and make a judgment regarding their
similarity as quickly as possible. It was found that the time required to make this judgment varied linearly according to the
three-dimensional angle separating the orientations of two views
of an identical object (see Figure 7-1). Not only was the degree

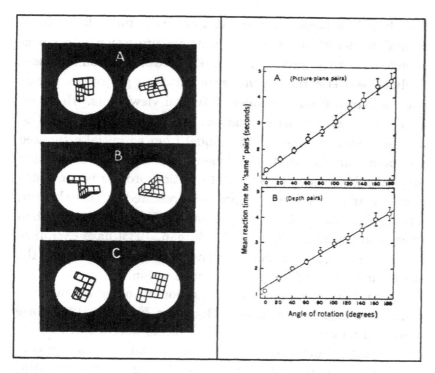

Figure 7-1: On the left are examples of the pairs of line drawings presented to subjects as described in [Shepard & Metzler, 1971]. The graphs on the right show the amount of time required to determine whether a pair of figures are rotationally equivalent. Graph A is for objects that were only rotated in the picture plane, and Graph B is for objects that were rotated in depth. [Reprinted with permission of the American Association for the Advancement of Science; Copyright 1971 by the AAAS.]

of linearity striking, but rotation in three-dimensions occurred at the same rate as rotation in the plane (this rate of rotation was roughly 60° per second). During the couple of seconds that it could take to complete the task, the subjects reported a strong subjective impression that they were mentally rotating one object until it matched the second.

This data seems to lend significant support to the hypothesis that viewpoint determination in human vision can be accomplished through a process of rotating a three-dimensional mental model of an object to bring its projection into correspondence with an image. The appearance of common objects is likely to be overlearned in the sense that their projected appearance is known from a number of typical viewpoints. However, for exact viewpoint determination, there would still need to be a small mental rotation of the model from an initial estimated viewpoint, and from unfamiliar viewpoints the required rotation may be substantial. This mental rotation process is conceptually similar to the iterative process presented in this chapter, although the method we will present has quadratic rather than linear convergence. [Funt, 1983; Morgan, 1983] have examined restrictions on computational architecture that could lead to the slower linear rate of rotation in human vision.

Note that viewpoint determination involves scaling and translation as well as rotation. [Bundesen & Larsen, 1975] have described an experiment in which subjects were asked to compare objects of differing size, and they found the same type of linear relationship between difference of scale and reaction time as was found for angle of rotation. It would be interesting to see whether there are similar experimental results for translation or variable model parameters.

7.2: Definition of the problem

In the simplest formulation, the problem will be to determine the orientation and position of a camera which would result in the projection of a given set of three-dimensional points into a given set of image points. Since there are six parameters determining orientation and location of the camera and since each match between an object point and an image point constrains two degrees of freedom, only three of these point-to-point matches are needed to achieve a complete solution (but there may still be a few discrete solutions). Although this aspect of the problem is not mathematically easy, a considerable amount of work has already been done on it as described in the next section.

However, the problem of matching object models to image features is usually substantially more complicated than is implied by this simple formulation. Our knowledge of objects is often not in terms of specific three-dimensional coordinates, but may involve many parameters of variation in object size, shape, or articulation. Since the spatial consequences of these parameters are confounded in the image with the effects of viewpoint, it is often necessary to solve simultaneously for viewpoint and model-specific parameters. In addition, the matches specified by the correspondences may not be in terms of points, but may instead be in terms of transverse distance from a model line to an image line or in terms of matches between more complex curves. This is particularly important for making use of current low-level edge detection methods which are much better at localizing the transverse position of a curve than in detecting the endpoints of a curve. A further important function of the verification process in developing practical vision systems is to remove positional errors from the initial set of matches by looking for consistent subsets with the most accurately determined parameters. A process which removes occasional incorrect matches can also greatly reduce the number of sets of correspondences which must be examined. These various extensions to the basic problem will all be addressed by the methods to be described in this chapter.

Let us consider for a moment the role of these mechanisms in a fairly difficult example of the verification problem. Imagine that we are trying to solve for viewpoint and model parameters in the case of recognizing a human figure. Although we know a great deal about the shape and structure of the human body, none of the dimensions are fixed in magnitude. Not only do people vary in every dimension of size and shape, but there are also numerous joints which can be articulated over a wide range of positions. However, many of the dimensions of variation are constrained to fairly narrow absolute or relative limits, and we have strong expectations for the bilateral symmetry of certain parameters. Given some tentative correspondences for say, the head, eyes and nose, we could use the expectation of bilateral symmetry and the mostly tightly constrained dimensions of our model to solve for approximate viewpoint. This would then suggest quite tightly constrained regions in which to search for other features, such as ears, neck, eyebrows, etc., each of which could be used to derive better estimates of viewpoint and the other parameters. An accurate determination for viewpoint and position of the head would then constrain the possible locations of the shoulders and arms, which could be predicted using mechanisms such as those in ACRONYM [Brooks, 1981]. In this chapter we will confine our attention to methods for solving for viewpoint and model parameters, making use of symmetry conditions, and extending the class of features which can be matched.

7.3: Previous research on viewpoint determination

The problem of solving for the six parameters of camera location and orientation given image locations for known three-dimensional points has received a considerable amount of attention in the field of photogrammetry. In photogrammetry this problem must be solved in order to use the positions of known landmarks in an aerial photograph to infer the ground coordinates of other parts of the image. One analytic solution to this problem—knows as the Church method—solves first for camera location and then orientation in a two-stage process. However, the first step of this process involves nonlinear equations which must be solved by an iterative numerical method. The current preferred method for solving this problem in the field of photogrammetry [Wolf, 1983] is an iterative method which solves for changes in all parameters simultaneously on each iteration, in a similar manner to the methods which will be presented in this chapter.

[Fischler & Bolles, 1981] present another closed-form solution for this problem and describe important results on the conditions under which multiple solutions exist for various numbers of correspondences between image and model. They establish that there are up to four solutions in the case of matching three points, and that multiple solutions may exist even for four or five matches in general position. This surprising result means that at least six matches of points in general position (a total of twelve constraints) is required to assure a unique solution to the six-parameter problem. The closed-form solution they present is quite complex and contains a quartic polynomial that presumably must be solved by iterative methods. However, these analytic results are useful on theoretical grounds. They may someday be extended to include model parameters, overdetermined systems, and forms of correspondence other than point-to-point matches, in which case they could replace the iterative methods used in this chapter. On the other hand, since the iterative methods are fast and typically require only two or three iterations, it is still not clear which would be most efficient.

[Ganapathy, 1984] describes a method for decomposing an already-given transformation matrix into the underlying camera parameters. Since this chapter is devoted to the problem of deriving the transformation matrix, Ganapathy's method could then be used to calculate camera parameters, including scaling and translation in the image plane, if these are desired. This is more likely of use as a camera calibration step than as an internal part of the recognition process.

7.4:   Formulation of perspective projection

Before the techniques for calculating the projection parameters can be presented, it is first necessary to define the methods and notation used for projection in the forward direction. The projection method presented here is similar to those which are commonly used for computer graphics. In essence, the technique is to specify a model of the camera being used and its location and orientation with respect to the three-dimensional model. These parameters are used in a coordinate transform to compute two-dimensional coordinates for points in the image from three-dimensional model coordinates.

The following transform models a standard camera with the lens pointing along a vector normal to the center of the image plane. The variable f specifies the distance of the image plane from the projection point, and usually does not need to be determined from the image when we are using a known camera (for convenience, we can let f represent the ratio of image distance to the width of the image plane, which means that image coordinates vary from 0 to 1 across the image). We must also specify a vector T giving the location of the camera lens in terms of world coordinates, and a rotation matrix R which depends on the camera orientation and maps points in world coordinates into points in a coordinate system with x and y axes parallel to the x and y axes of the camera film plane. Then the transform

$$(x, y, z) = R(p - T)$$

$$(x', y') = \left(\frac{fx}{z}, \frac{fy}{z} \right)$$

first transforms the point p in world coordinates into the point (x, y, z) in camera-based coordinates, and then creates the perspective projection of this point onto the image plane, with image coordinates (x', y').

The most difficult aspect of the transformation is representing and working with the rotation R. Most work in computer graphics chooses to represent rotations with three-by-three matrices, but this representation is not very good for our purposes since it uses nine variables to represent something which has only three underlying parameters. Another possibility is to represent the rotation by giving its axis of rotation plus the angle of rotation about this axis. In fact, we can let the magnitude

of the axis vector represent the magnitude of the rotation, and
we have thus reduced the rotation to the minimal three parameters. However, the axis-angle representation requires a good
deal of computation when we actually wish to rotate a point,
and also makes it difficult to compose rotations. Quaternions
[Salamin, 1979] are a representation which combine the advantages of these other methods and have proved to be the most
useful for our work. They use four variables to represent a rotation in such a way that composition, normalization, rotation,
and creation of a rotation about an arbitrary axis are all computationally efficient. Although the implementation which will
be described uses quaternions, the solution we will give to the
viewpoint determination problem is independent of any particular representation for rotations.

7.5: Newton-Raphson convergence

There are seven underlying parameters in the camera transform
presented above: three parameters give the camera position T,
three more are sufficient to specify the rotation R, and f specifies
a property of the camera itself. In addition, there can be any
number of parameters specifying variations in the model. Our
problem is to calculate the values for these parameters which
produce the best fit between an image and the projection of
a model. Although we have mentioned work on developing an
analytic solution, it seems that an iterative solution is currently
the best alternative in terms of generality and efficiency. The
method we have chosen is Newton-Raphson convergence, which
has a fast quadratic convergence and can be cleanly applied to
this problem. This technique works best when the derivatives
are all fairly independent of one another and are smooth enough
over the error range for good convergence.

Unfortunately, the specification of the camera transform
given in the previous section does not have simple derivatives
of x' and y' with respect to the camera transform parameters.

Once again, this is a result of the fact that it is difficult to represent a rotation in terms of its three underlying parameters. This difficulty can be eliminated by reparameterizing the camera transform to express it in terms of parameters that are related to the camera coordinate system rather than world coordinates. This new transform must be chosen carefully from among the various possibilities in order to keep the parameters as independent as possible from each other and to keep the derivatives simple. As before, our new transform specifies how a three-dimensional point p is to be mapped onto a point in the image (x', y'):

$$(x, y, z) = R(p)$$

$$(x', y') = \left(\frac{fx}{z + D_z} + D_x, \; \frac{fy}{z + D_z} + D_y \right)$$

$$= (fxc + D_x, \; fyc + D_y) \text{ where } c = \frac{1}{z + D_z}$$

Here the variables R and f remain the same as in the previous transform, but the vector T has been replaced by (D_x, D_y, D_z), where the two transforms are equivalent when

$$T = R^{-1} \left(-\frac{D_x(z + D_z)}{f}, \; -\frac{D_y(z + D_z)}{f}, \; -D_z \right)$$

The new parameterization is much better for our purposes, since D_x and D_y simply specify the location of the object on the image plane and D_z specifies the distance of the object from the camera. Compare this with the very indirect specification of these same camera-related variables given by T. However, we have still solved only half the problem, since the three parameters underlying the rotation matrix are still difficult to express in a form closely related to the image. Our solution to this second problem was not to try to somehow express R in terms of image-centered parameters, but to take the initial specification

	x	y	z
ϕ_x	0	$-z$	y
ϕ_y	z	0	$-x$
ϕ_z	$-y$	x	0

Figure 7-2: Partial derivatives of x, y and z with respect to counter-clockwise rotations ϕ's (in radians) about the coordinate axes.

of R as given and add to it incremental rotations ϕ_x, ϕ_y and ϕ_z about the x, y and z axes of the *camera* coordinate system. It is easy to compose rotations (and particularly efficient when the quaternion representation of rotations is used as mentioned above), and the incremental rotations are fairly independent of one another if they are small. The Newton-Raphson method is now carried out by correcting errors in x' and y' by calculating the optimum correction rotations ϕ_x, ϕ_y and ϕ_z to be made about the image axes. Instead of adding these corrections to underlying parameters of R we create rotations of the given magnitudes about their respective coordinate axes and compose these new rotations with R.

One major advantage of using the ϕ's as our convergence parameters is that the derivatives of x, y, and z (and therefore of x' and y') with respect to them can be expressed in a strikingly simple form. For example, the derivative of x at a point (x, y) with respect to a counter-clockwise rotation of ϕ_z about the z axis is simply $-y$, since $(x, y) = (d\cos\phi_z, d\sin\phi_z)$ and therefore $\partial x / \partial \phi_z = -d\sin\phi_z = -y$. The table in Figure 7-2 gives these derivatives for all combinations of values.

Given these derivatives it is straightforward to accomplish our original objective of calculating the partial derivatives of x' and y' with respect to each of the original camera parameters. For example, our transform tells us that:

	x'	y'
D_x	1	0
D_y	0	1
D_z	$-fc^2x$	$-fc^2y$
ϕ_x	$-fc^2xy$	$-fc(z+cy^2)$
ϕ_y	$fc(z+cx^2)$	fc^2xy
ϕ_z	$-fcy$	fcx
f	cx	cy

Figure 7-3: Partial derivatives of x' and y' with respect to each of the camera transform parameters.

$$x' = \frac{fx}{z+D_z} + D_x$$

so

$$\frac{\partial x'}{\partial D_x} = 1$$

and

$$\frac{\partial x'}{\partial \phi_y} = \frac{f}{z+D_z}\frac{\partial x}{\partial \phi_y} - \frac{fx}{(z+D_z)^2}\frac{\partial z}{\partial \phi_y}$$

$$= fcz + fc^2x^2 = fc(z+cx^2)$$

and

$$\frac{\partial x'}{\partial \phi_z} = \frac{f}{z+D_z}\frac{\partial x}{\partial \phi_z} = -fcy.$$

All the other derivatives can be calculated in a similar way, and the table in Figure 7-3 gives the derivatives of x' and y' with respect to each of the seven parameters of our camera model.

Given these partial derivatives of x' and y', it is easy to perform the convergence. For each point in the model which should match against some corresponding point in the image, we first calculate the camera transform of the model point and measure the error in its x component when compared to the given image point. We then create an equation which expresses this error E as the sum of the products of its partial derivatives times the error correction values:

$$\frac{\partial x'}{\partial D_x}\Delta D_x + \frac{\partial x'}{\partial D_y}\Delta D_y + \frac{\partial x'}{\partial D_z}\Delta D_z + \frac{\partial x'}{\partial \phi_x}\Delta \phi_x$$

$$+ \frac{\partial x'}{\partial \phi_y}\Delta \phi_y + \frac{\partial x'}{\partial \phi_z}\Delta \phi_z = E$$

Using the same point we create a similar equation for its y component, so for each point correspondence we derive two equations. From three point correspondences we can derive six equations and produce a complete linear system which can be solved for all six camera model corrections (we are assuming in this example that the camera parameter f is either given, or can be approximated by a large value). After each iteration the Δ terms should shrink by about one order of magnitude, and no more than a few iterations should be needed even for high accuracy.

In most applications of this method we will be given more correspondences between model and image than are strictly necessary, and we will want to perform some kind of best fit. In this case the Gauss least-squares method can easily be applied. The matrix equation given above can be expressed as

$$[A][\Delta] = [E]$$

where $[A]$ is the derivative matrix, $[\Delta]$ is the vector of unknown corrections, and $[E]$ is the vector of error terms. When this system is overdetermined, we can perform a least-squares fit of the errors simply by solving

$$[A]^T[A][\Delta] = [A]^T[E]$$

where $[A]^T[A]$ is square and has the correct dimensions for the vector $[\Delta]$.

The convergence properties of this solution are such that there should be few problems in picking the initial parameter values from which to converge. As long as the rotation errors ϕ_x, ϕ_y and ϕ_z are not greater than about 45 degrees, almost any values can be chosen for the other parameters. Usually, the source of the hypothesized matches carries a rough implication of the orientation of the object—for example, the search methods described in the previous chapter break the range of orientations down into smaller sets, so that approximate viewpoint is known for any final match.

7.6: Solving for model parameters

We have been describing the process of solving for the parameters which determine an object's position and orientation with respect to the external world. An important extension to this method is the ability to use models which are parameterized internally, and have variable parts or articulations between parts. We can determine the values of these model parameters in the same way that we determine the correct projection parameters. The only requirement is that we be able to calculate the directional derivatives of points in the model with respect to the new parameters. For the common types of model parameterization, such as variable lengths or variable rotations about some axis, these derivatives are easily determined in closed form. For other forms of parameterization, a simple numerical technique which slightly perturbs the parameter and measures the resulting change in the image can be used to determine the derivative. These derivatives can then be used in the same way for convergence as were those for the other parameters. We will now require more given correspondences between image and model in order to have a fully-determined system, but since each additional correspondence between an image point and a model point allows us to solve for two more unknown variables there should be little difficulty in meeting this requirement.

The power of this method can be best illustrated by giving an example. Assume that we want to recognize images of
different types of airplanes, and we do not know in advance
which type of airplane will be in a certain image. In this
case our airplane model will have to be quite general and will
not be able to give precise measurements for various lengths
or such things as the angle between the wings and the fuse-
lage. However, certain important constraints are known, such
as the fact that the airplane will be symmetrical about the fuse-
lage. This symmetry will be represented to the convergence
algorithm by the fact that the model parameters referring to
the right wing will be the same as those referring to the left
wing, and any changes in these parameters refer to both wings.
The convergence algorithm will then determine a camera transform and wing-fuselage angle which together produce the closest
fit of model to image, as in the example in Figure 7-5. Note
that there may well be insufficient information to determine
either the camera transform or the wing-fuselage angle independently, so the ability to solve for both simultaneously using
knowledge of the airplane's symmetry is crucial to determining
a solution.

Another form of constraint arises when we have some prior
knowledge about the location of an object. For example, we
may know the position of the ground plane relative to the
camera and we can constrain the airplane to be positioned
on the ground. In this case the airplane has only three degrees of freedom in its position (its x and y location on the
ground and its orientation about the vertical axis). In this
situation we do not need to solve for the full camera model,
since this has already been determined relative to the ground
plane. Instead, we can just solve for the parameters giving the position of the airplane relative to the ground using the techniques given above. This suggests that a more
uniform description of the viewpoint-determination algorithm
would be to treat the parameters which we have been calling

"projection parameters" as just other kinds of model parameters which give the position of the entire object relative to camera space.

7.7: Matching lines instead of points

Another important extension to the basic algorithm is to allow it to use line-to-line correspondences in addition to point-to-point ones. This is important in practice because low-level vision routines are relatively good at finding the transverse locations of lines but are much less certain about exactly where the lines terminate. What we need to do is express our errors in terms of the distance of one line from another, rather than in terms of the error in the locations of points. The solution we have adopted is to measure as our errors the perpendicular distance of each endpoint of the model line from the corresponding line in the image, and to then take the derivatives in terms of this distance rather than in terms of x' or y'. This the appropriate constraint mathematically—that the model line should lie on top of the image line but that the endpoints need not correspond. In order to express the perpendicular distance of a point from a line it is useful to first express the line as an equation of the following form, in which m is the slope:

$$\frac{-m}{\sqrt{m^2 + 1}}\, x + \frac{1}{\sqrt{m^2 + 1}}\, y = d$$

In this equation d is the perpendicular distance of the line from the origin. If we substitute some point (x', y') into the left side of the equation and calculate the new value of d for this point (call it d'), then the perpendicular distance of this point from the line is simply $d - d'$. What is more, it is easy to calculate the derivatives of d' for use in the convergence, since the derivatives of d' are just a linear combination of the derivatives of x' and y' as given in the above equation, and we already know how to calculate the x' and y' derivatives from the solution given for using point correspondences. The result is that each line-to-line correspondence we are given between model and image gives us two equations for our linear system—the same amount of information that is conveyed by a point-to-point correspondence.

7.8: Implementation and future research

The full viewpoint determination method and extensions described above have been implemented in MACLISP on a DEC KL-10 computer. The algorithm has performed reliably and usually converges to the correct transform and parameter values to within about 1 part in 10^4 in less than 4 iterations. When solving simultaneously for six or seven parameters and making use of 10 to 15 matches in the image, each iteration executes in about 20 milliseconds. Another implementation of the algorithm, as a part of the SCERPO vision system, will be described in the next chapter.

The example shown in Figure 7-4 makes use of models from the ACRONYM vision system [Brooks, 1981]. Although ACRONYM allows its models to be extensively parameterized, in this case all parameters of the model are fixed in value to represent an L1011 passenger plane. Correspondences are specified between some two-dimensional lines in the image plane and three-dimensional edges of the model, and rough initial estimates of the camera parameters are given. As shown, the algorithm then converges to the best least-squares estimate of viewpoint within about three iterations. Note that the endpoints of the image lines are not forced to match the endpoints of the model lines, since the algorithm only attempts to minimize the perpendicular distance between the edges. The standard deviation of the errors remaining after the least-squares process is an indication of the consistency and therefore the correctness of the original match. More significantly, the model now makes many predictions for further edges at specific locations in the image, which can be searched for in order to perform

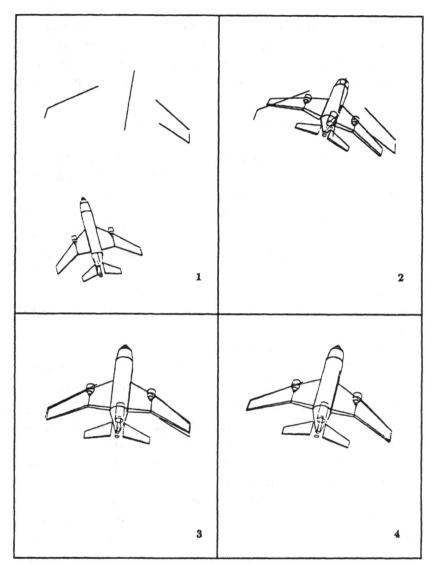

Figure 7-4: The three-dimensional model of the airplane is from the ACRONYM vision system. The initial estimate of position and orientation is shown in the box at the upper left, and the program is also given correspondences between edges in the model and the displayed two-dimensional lines. The first three iterations of convergence towards a least-squares solution of viewpoint are shown in the other boxes. Note that endpoints of image lines are not forced to correspond with endpoints in the model.

further verification or increase the accuracy of the viewpoint determination.

Figure 7-5 is an example of solving for model parameters simultaneously with viewpoint. The airplane model is parameterized so that the wings can be swept back and forth, and the same parameter is used for both wings so that the model is constrained to be symmetric. There is not enough information in the given correspondences to solve for either viewpoint or the wing sweep independently, so it is only the capability for simultaneous solution that enables the problem to be solved. This is a common example of the way in which viewpoint and model parameters can be confounded in the spatial information of an image.

This algorithm has also recently been applied in a successful commercial vision system [Goad, 1983]. After some initial edge matches have been found by a fast search process, the viewpoint-determination is used for final verification and determination of precise position.

There are a number of other potentially useful extensions to this algorithm. After producing the least-squares fit for overdetermined data, it would be useful if the algorithm could then use the extra information to throw out those points which are least consistent with the others. The easiest method would be to discard points or lines with the highest residual errors and to reconverge on the remaining ones. This procedure can fail when there are gross errors, in which case the RANSAC method [Fischler & Bolles, 1981] may be the most appropriate. However, for the matching techniques described in the previous chapter, the errors in correspondence may be always small enough to make this unnecessary.

There is also further work to be done at the level of integrating this method with other components of a vision system. Given a model, the various unknown parameters, and a set of correspondences between model and image features, there could be a supervisory procedure which selects which parameters to

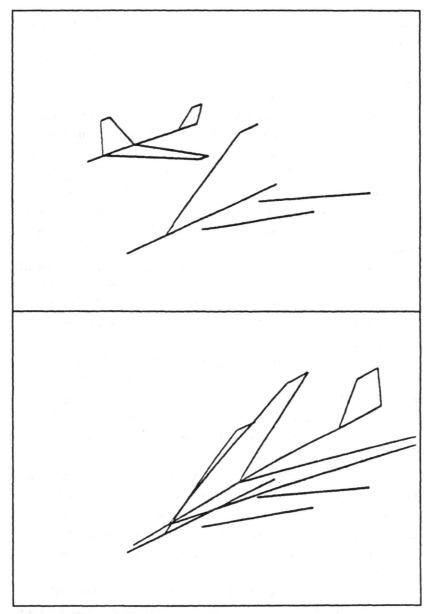

Figure 7-5(a,b): The simple airplane model in this example is parameterized so that the wings can sweep back and forth while maintaining the bilateral symmetry of the model. The algorithm can solve for the wing sweep simultaneously with solving for viewpoint.

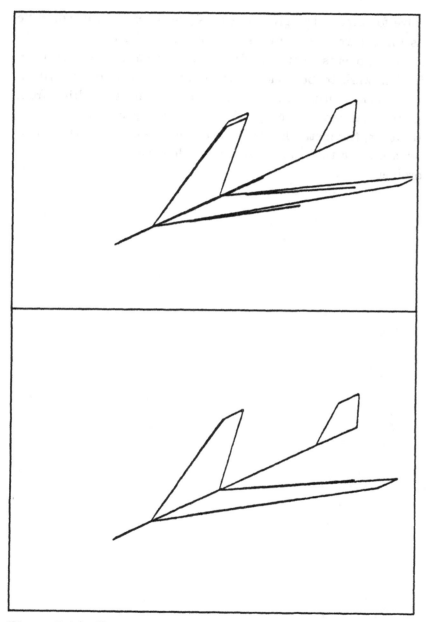

Figure 7-5(c,d): These figures show the second and third iterations of convergence while solving for viewpoint and wing-sweep parameters. Convergence to the limits of accuracy of the data typically takes no more than three or four iterations.

solve for first. Also, given a least-squares solution, it would be useful to carry the resulting error estimates back to the matching components for use in further predictions. There is much further work to be done on the remaining aspects of verification, such as using the region correspondences resulting from spatial matching to verify color, texture or shading properties. However, the methods which have been presented in this chapter are more than sufficient for a wide class of common vision problems.

Chapter 8

THE SCERPO
VISION SYSTEM

THE PREVIOUS CHAPTERS have described a number of separate components that would need to function together to perform visual recognition. In this chapter, an implemented vision system will be described that combines many of these components into a functioning system for performing recognition. The system has been named SCERPO (an acronym for Spatial Correspondence, Evidential Reasoning, and Perceptual Organization). All code for this system was written over a relatively short period by a single person, which required that each component be simplified over the more complete versions previously described. For example, curve segmentation is performed only for straight line segments rather than arbitrary curves, object models are presumed to be fully specified with no unknown internal parameters, perceptual organization has been simplified, and the evidential reasoning component does little more than an exhaustive search. Nevertheless, the system has a high level of performance in comparison to most previous vision systems, and it clearly demonstrates the potential for the methodology as a whole. The SCERPO system provides a working framework for incorporating numerous improvements at all levels, and it is hoped that the reader will leave this chapter with a clear sense of the potential opportunities for further research and implementation.

Before examining the methods used in SCERPO, we should briefly review the history of previous implementations of model-based vision systems. The remarkable early work of [Roberts, 1966] demonstrated the recognition of certain polyhedral objects by exactly solving for viewpoint and object parameters. Matching was performed by searching for correspondences between junctions found in the scene and junctions of model edges. Verification was then based upon exact solution of viewpoint and model parameters using a method that required seven point-to-point correspondences. Unfortunately, this work was poorly incorporated into later vision research, which instead tended to emphasize non-quantitative and less general methods such as line-labeling. The ACRONYM system [Brooks, 1981] has been discussed extensively in Chapter 6. It used a general symbolic constraint solver to calculate bounds on viewpoint and model parameters. While providing an influential and very general framework, the actual calculation of bounds for such general constraints was mathematically difficult and approximations were used that did not lead to exact solutions for viewpoint. Matching was performed by looking for particular types of elongated structures in the image (known as ribbons) and matching them to potentially corresponding parts of the model. The system described in [Goad, 1983] was also discussed in detail in Chapter 6. By using a system of extensive precomputation for each particular object to be recognized, this system is able to calculate the relevant bounds extremely quickly at runtime. A further advantage is that it needs to perform edge-detection only within the predicted bounds at the minimum required resolution. A version of the algorithm implemented at Silma Incorporated has demonstrated object recognition within a couple of seconds on a single microprocessor, including edge detection.

For this reason, this technique will probably continue to be the method of choice for industrial systems in which only a small number of objects need to be recognized. Some other successful model-based vision systems, based on rather different techniques, are described in [Shirai, 1978; and Walter & Tropf, 1983]. We will now examine the SCERPO system, which makes use of perceptual organization and a general, quantitative method for achieving spatial correspondence.

8.1: Edge detection

This book has made no attempt to break new ground at the level of detecting primitive intensity discontinuities in an image. Likewise, the SCERPO vision system uses established methods to perform the first few steps of image processing. Figures 8-1 to 8-3 show the application of the basic zero-crossing methods of [Marr & Hildreth, 1980] that were used in the first stages of the SCERPO system. The 512×512 pixel image shown in Figure 8-1(a) was convolved with a Laplacian of Gaussian function ($\sigma = 1.8$ pixels) to yield the results shown in Figure 8-1(b). The intensity of each point in Figure 8-1(b) is proportional to the absolute value of the result of the convolution, so that values near zero are black.

The processing was performed on a VICOM image processor using the *Vsh* software facility developed by [Clark & Hummel, 1984]. The VICOM can perform a 3×3 convolution against the entire image in a single video frame time. The *Vsh* software facility allowed the 18×18 convolution kernel required for our purposes to be automatically decomposed into 36 of the 3×3 primitive convolutions along with the appropriate image translations and additions. More efficient implementations which apply a smaller Laplacian convolution kernel to the image followed by iterated Gaussian blur were rejected due to their numerical imprecision.

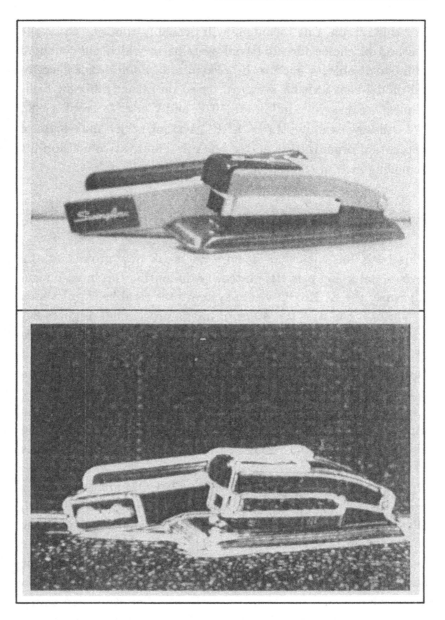

Figure 8-1: (a) The original image, taken by a CCD camera at a resolution of 512×512 pixels. (b) Convolution of the image with the $\nabla^2 G$ function ($\sigma = 1.8$ pixels). Intensity is proportional to the absolute value of the convolution.

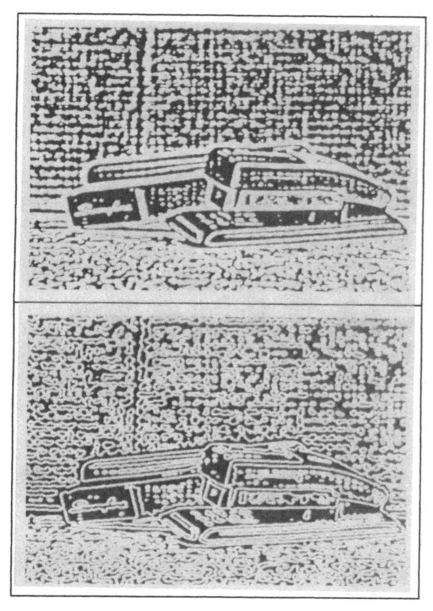

Figure 8-2: (a) Thresholded $\nabla^2 G$ image, with positive regions shown white and negative regions black. (b) Zero crossings formed along the boundaries between white and black regions of the thresholded image.

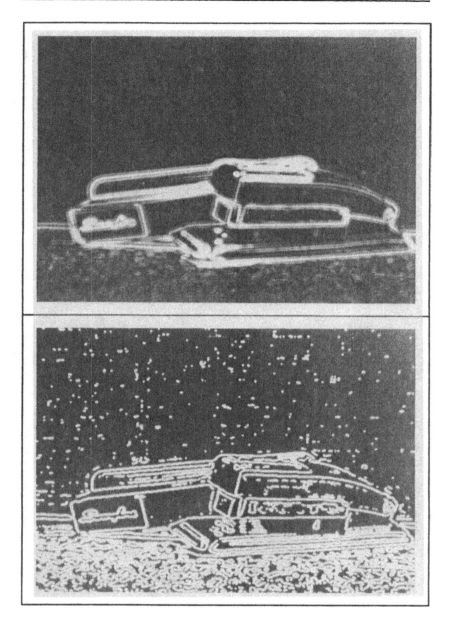

Figure 8-3: (a) Result of applying the Sobel gradient operator to the $\nabla^2 G$ image of Figure 8-1(b). (b) Selection of those zero crossing pixels that are above a given threshold in the Sobel gradient image.

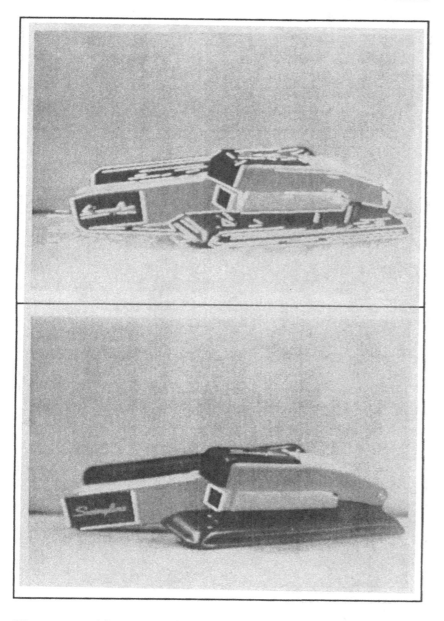

Figure 8-4: (a) Result after linking of zero-crossings and selection of most significant straight-line segmentations. (b) The two perceptual groupings that were actually used for the successful recognition (about 200 other groupings were formed).

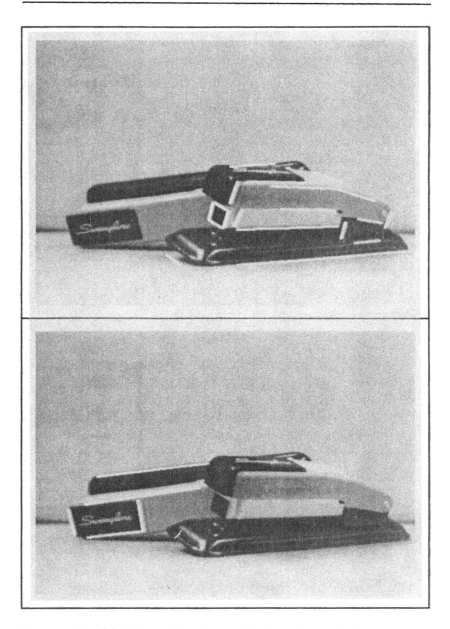

Figure 8-5: (a) After solving for model viewpoint, selecting new segments most consistent with model predictions, and iterating, these segments were selected as being consistent with one projection of the model. (b) The segments for a second projection.

Figure 8-6: (a) The model superimposed on the image from the final calculated viewpoint. (b) The same model shown from the second calculated viewpoint. Slight orientation error is due to measurement error in the image and small amount of data being used.

Figure 8-2(a) shows the image of 8-1(b) thresholded into positive and negative regions. Figure 8-2(b) shows only the zero-crossings along the boundaries between these regions. Of course, many of these zero-crossings do not correspond to significant edges in the image. We can remove those corresponding to insignificant intensity changes by measuring the gradient of the $\nabla^2 G$ convolution, as suggested in [Marr & Hildreth, 1980]. Figure 8-3(a) shows the results of applying the Sobel gradient operator to the $\nabla^2 G$ convolution of Figure 8-1(b). Only those pixels that are above a chosen gradient threshold in Figure 8-3(a) and lie on a zero-crossing are retained in Figure 8-3(b). This image is then transferred from the VICOM to a general-purpose VAX computer, and these remaining zero-crossings are linked into lists of points on the basis of connectivity. In the future, we plan to retain the gradient measurement for each point along a zero-crossing and to select for significance only after linking and other operations have been performed.

8.2: Perceptual organization

The first stage of perceptual organization, as described in Chapter 4, is to derive meaningful curve descriptions from the list of edge points. However, the general methods of Chapter 4 have been greatly simplified in this implementation. We look only for straight-line segmentations and only select the highest significance representation at each point along the curve. The significance of a straight line fit to a list of points is measured as simply the ratio of its length divided by the maximum deviation of a point from the line. A lower limit is placed on the minimum measurable deviation according to the resolution of the image, so that significance cannot become infinite. This provides a scale-independent measure of significance that places no prior bounds on the allowable deviations. This is then used in a modified version of the recursive endpoint subdivision method. A segment is subdivided at the point with maximum deviation from a line connecting its endpoints. If the maximum significance of the subsegments is greater than the significance of the complete segment, then the subsegments are returned. Otherwise the single segment is returned. The procedure will return a segment covering every point along the curve, but only those with significance ratio above 4 are retained. This method is implemented in only 40 lines of lisp code, yet does a reasonable job of detecting the most perceptually significant straight line groupings in the linked point data. The results are shown in Figure 8-4(a). Previous researchers have pointed out that the recursive subdivision method may sometimes subdivide at an incorrect point. However, an occasional extra subdivision will often be reconnected during later collinearity detection.

We have chosen only three primitive relations for the implementation of perceptual grouping. These are collinearity, proximity of endpoints, and parallelism. The straight line segments are indexed according to endpoint locations and orientation. Then a sequence of procedures is executed to detect instances of the primitive relations. A region around each endpoint or segment is examined to determine candidates for grouping. Each potential grouping is assigned a significance value that is roughly inversely proportional to the likelihood that it is accidental in origin. This is done in a scale-independent manner, meaning that measurements of endpoint proximity or separation of parallel lines are divided by the length of the shortest of the two line segments to determine significance. After the execution of this grouping process, each line segment points to lists of other line segments satisfying the various relations with it with varying levels of significance. Unfortunately, it is difficult to display the results of this grouping process without showing a separate image for each grouping that has been detected. Although several hundred significant groupings were detected among the line segments of Figure 8-4(a), we show in Figure 8-4(b) only the two sets of groupings that were actually used for successful recognition.

8.3: Matching and evidential reasoning

The evidential reasoning component of SCERPO is currently less developed than the other parts of the system. Since the system has only been used with a single object under consideration, the performance requirements for minimizing search have not been great. The system makes use of a list of perceptual groupings and the model features that could give rise to them. Currently, this list is entered by hand at the same time as model specification. Each grouping consists of only a few line segments, and only a few groupings need to be entered for each side of the model to assure a reasonable chance for recognition. For example, the groupings shown in Figure 8-4(b) consist of particular combinations of parallelism and endpoint proximity that could be matched to various parts of the object model. Some groupings are better than others for viewpoint determination. For example, there are a large number of highly significant instances of parallelism in the images, but they are not used in isolation for matching since a series of parallel line segments does not offer complete restriction on viewpoint and would either take more time to verify or fail to result in a solution. The probabilities of non-accidentalness for the image relations that make up a grouping are multiplied together to calculate the probability for the grouping as a whole. This is multiplied by an estimate of the likelihood of correctness for the match that has been entered for each element of the association list, and these final values are used to order the search.

In further research, we plan to explore methods for learning the associations between groupings and corresponding parts of objects and also for learning the required probability values. Once an object has been recognized, it is possible to return to the image data structure and look for high-significance groupings that have been projected by the model. Probabilistic values for these associations, as described in Chapter 6, can be incrementally modified towards their correct values by keeping track of the associations across many instances of recognition. Therefore, it seems quite possible to create a system that will gradually increase its reliability and speed of operation as it gains experience in seeing a particular object. This would also lead to the creation of far more potential sets of matches for initiating the recognition of each object, and would therefore improve performance when large numbers of object features are occluded or otherwise missing.

8.4: Verification

In many ways, it is the verification module that is the most powerful component of the current system. This module is able to take a tentative match between a couple of image features and model features and return a reliable answer as to whether the match is correct. If the object is present, this module will extend the match as much as possible and determine the precise viewpoint.

The verification proceeds by making use of the few initial matches to precisely solve for viewpoint, using the mathematical methods given in Chapter 7. If the problem is overconstrained, then a least-squares fit is performed. The calculated viewpoint can then be used to derive many further predictions for the locations of model features in the image. Given errors in image measurements, it is necessary to examine a range of image locations around each prediction for possible matches. However, false matches can be minimized by ranking all the possible matches according to their lack of ambiguity and selecting only those that are least ambiguous for each iteration of viewpoint determination. Each potential match between a projected model feature and image feature is evaluated according to the accuracy of agreement in position, length, and orientation, as well as according to the lack of competing matches. Therefore, in ambiguous cases such as occur when there are many closely-spaced

parallel lines in the image, the selection of the best match is de-
layed until most other features have been matched and used to
determine the best possible least-squares estimate of viewpoint.
One final method used to decrease ambiguity is applied to instances of an extremal edge of the model (i.e., an edge such that
all features of the model projected from the current viewpoint
fall on only one side of the edge). In this instance, the ambiguity measure is decreased when matching the extremal edge to
an edge in the image that has no other nearby parallel lines in
the extremal direction. Once again, this sometimes helps to select the correct match when there are many parallel edges close
together in the image.

Figure 8-5 shows the set of line segments that were selected
as being consistent with a particular viewpoint of the model
following the iterative verification procedure. Figure 8-6 shows
the model from the final best-fit viewpoint superimposed on the
image. The same model was used for both instances of the
stapler in the image. The model consists simply of straight 3-
D line segments, with visibility information attached to each
segment. The visibility information consists of a list of 3-D
vectors, such that if the dot-product of the camera position with
any vector is positive, then the line segment is visible. This
provides a very crude form of hidden-line elimination, but is
one that can be calculated very quickly. The verification would
improve if a full hidden-line algorithm were used, particularly
for the case of occlusion between objects.

There are many further extensions that could be made to
increase the reliability and accuracy of the viewpoint determination. Since the solution is often greatly overdetermined, it is
possible to throw out points with the greatest residual errors
after a least-squares fit and reconverge on the remaining data.
This would allow "noise" points to be removed and would result
in an increase in final accuracy of viewpoint. It would greatly
decrease ambiguity if more information were available from the
model, such as the approximate contrast ratios across particular

edges. In fact, once viewpoint is known, it is comparatively easy to make use of many surface properties such as color, shading, and texture measures for final verification. The current implementation makes use of only the crude segmented image data for verification, whereas much greater accuracy and further correspondences could be achieved by returning to the zero-crossings or original image.

8.5: System performance and future extensions

The SCERPO system is written in several different languages. The image processing components are executed on a VICOM Image Processor as described in the section on edge detection. The zero-crossing image is then transferred to a VAX 11/750 running UNIX BSD 4.2 for subsequent processing. A program written in C reads the original image and produces a file of linked edge points (requiring about 30 seconds of CPU time). All other components are written in Franz Lisp. Segmentation into straight line segments requires 40 seconds, indexing and grouping operations require about 1 minute and the later stages of matching and verification took 40 seconds for this example, while running on the low-end VAX 11/750 computer. The VAX operations will soon be moved to a PYRAMID computer, which will decrease execution times by a substantial factor. We are also exploring the possibility of executing the code on an eight-processor prototype of the NYU Ultracomputer [Gottlieb *et al.*, 1983] available in our laboratory, which runs a parallel version of the UNIX operating system. Further improvements could be obtained by calling efficient numeric subroutines externally from the Franz Lisp code (Franz Lisp currently forces all floating point operations to be performed in double precision).

The current capabilities of SCERPO provide a framework that could be used to incorporate numerous additional capabilities. A brief list of some of these possible extensions would include the following: incorporation of zero-crossings detected at multiple scales, more extensive use of the zero-crossing gradient, the detection of significant curve segments as well as straight lines, use of least-squares to fit segments to edge points, use of a wider range of perceptual grouping operations, the ability to handle variable object parameters, the recognition of object components and their subsequent combination, more complete modeling with surface information and hidden-line algorithms, the expanded use of evidential reasoning, the incremental learning of grouping associations and probabilities, and the incorporation of color and texture information. Each of these topics has either been discussed in this book or has been demonstrated in the computer vision literature. Given a solid level of performance in the existing system, each added capability would be required to prove its usefulness according to its ability to expand the generality of the system or improve performance.

Chapter 9
CONCLUSIONS

W E ARE now in a position to look back over the range of material in this book and evaluate its contributions to computer vision research. The direction that has been taken is substantially different from the mainstream of current computer vision research. Our goal at the outset was to develop methods for visual recognition based upon the use of spatial information in the image. The direct formation of depth information from the image has been de-emphasized, and a process of perceptual organization has taken its place as a primary bottom-up descriptive process. The problem of visual recognition has been cast as essentially a problem of search, in which the major research effort needs to be devoted to reducing the size of the search space at each level of the visual hierarchy. A consequence of this search-based methodology is that intermediate levels of description are not required to be highly reliable; rather, it is their average statistical performance in distinguishing useful alternatives which is of importance for reducing the search space. This naturally leads to methods for evaluating relations which are probabilistic in nature rather than being based upon binary decisions.

149

Some parts of this methodology have been developed to a much greater extent than others. Fortunately, the most crucial component upon which the search-based methodology relies—the ability to make a reliable final judgment regarding the correctness of an interpretation—is one of the most completely developed components. The method presented in Chapter 7 for using a few initial matches to determine spatial correspondence is fast, reliable, and operates to the limits of accuracy in the data. It also provides a basis for examining correspondence of region-based measures, such as color, texture or shading. Although the method works for parameterized models of an object, further extensions would be required to apply the method to objects with poorly defined structure.

A major portion of this book has been devoted to the use of perceptual organization as a bottom-up process for structuring the spatial information in an image, with the end goal of using these structures to reduce the size of the search space during recognition. This objective led to the requirement that algorithms for perceptual organization be designed to distinguish significant structural relations as reliably as possible from those which arise by accident. Chapter 3 presented a number of important criteria derived from this requirement which must be taken into account in the design of any algorithms for perceptual organization. These criteria provide a unified basis for the problem of perceptual organization, even though there may be a large collection of separate algorithms for carrying out the component processes. The component of perceptual organization which was chosen for the most extensive investigation was the problem of segmenting two-dimensional image curves. This is an important problem for many other aspects of organization, and the algorithm which was developed has the capability of detecting significant structure wherever it occurs at multiple scales of resolution. Another component which was investigated in some detail was the process of inferring curve categorizations and three-dimensional relations from perceptual groupings. However, the topic of perceptual organization covers a very large number of capabilities, and these components must be considered as only first steps.

The SCERPO vision system provides a working demonstration of the methodology, although it implements only a fraction of the potential capabilities. However, enough has been implemented to provide a strong degree of support for this direction of research and to demonstrate the current practicality of systems based on these methods.

9.1: Directions for future development

The search-based methodology for recognition provides an attractive route for the incremental development of computer vision systems with improved capabilities. It is possible right now to build model-based vision systems which can operate well in domains with small numbers of well-specified objects. We can expect improved performance from further development of any of the underlying components of this methodology.

As new methods of perceptual organization are developed, we can expect significant decreases in the size of this search space. The extent of this decrease provides a well-specified criterion for evaluating the success of proposed improvements in algorithms for perceptual organization. We can hope that the many components of perceptual organization will yield to common techniques and that it is unnecessary to explore separate algorithms for each form of grouping or description. The goal of identifying non-accidentalness provides a unifying objective for these many processes. However, current neurophysiological evidence regarding the human visual system seems to indicate that there are many different modules for carrying out the different descriptive processes, so there may be a large number of separate problems which must be solved. Fortunately, the highly redundant and overconstrained nature of visual information means that useful performance can be achieved long before all these problems are solved.

Another topic for further research is the integration of depth information with the two-dimensional perceptual grouping operations. We have paid little attention to this topic, possibly in an overreaction to the previous emphasis on the direct derivation of depth information as a prerequisite to recognition. Clearly, motion and stereo correspondence provide a useful source of quantitative constraints which can be used to limit the search required for recognition. They are particularly important when the recognition process breaks down, as when encountering a completely unfamiliar object for the first time. Perceptual organization can operate as well in three dimensions as it can in two, and this can be an important aspect of learning the most natural description for a new object. In the reverse direction, perceptual groupings and recognition can be important components for establishing correspondence for motion and stereo. To the extent that perceptual groupings are non-accidental in origin and invariant with respect to viewpoint, we can expect them to be present in a sequence of different views of a scene. These groupings provide far less ambiguous descriptions for matching than do lower-level image features.

The methods for model-based verification that were presented in Chapter 7 could be extended in a number of directions. Once the determination of spatial correspondence has been performed, it is possible to examine correspondence between region-based properties such as color, shading, or texture. Methods need to be developed for measuring and comparing each of these properties. Another direction for the development of verification is to allow greater variation in object models. The simple forms of continuous parameterization that have been described are only a start in this direction. It is necessary to model not only individual objects but also the typical relations between objects that are expected in a coherent scene. New forms of object modeling must be developed as well as ways to carry out the search and verification processes with these types of models.

One of the most exciting areas for further research is the development of evidential reasoning and related methods for automatically learning associations between evidence and interpretations. These methods show promise for carrying out the longstanding objective of combining many sources of information in a flexible way to achieve recognition. Just as important is the potential for building learning systems which improve their performance as they accumulate visual experience. The use of evidential reasoning would greatly facilitate the incremental incorporation of new research results in image description, object modeling, and verification.

Finally, there is much room for development in the areas of improved computational hardware and methods for handling large quantities of information. It is often remarked that vision requires a large amount of computational power. It is much less common to note that vision also places extreme demands on the amount of knowledge that a system needs to retain and access. Human memory continues to accumulate new information regarding the visual appearance of objects and their arrangement in scenes throughout decades of visual exposure during almost every waking moment. Experiments with visual memory indicate that the human brain probably contains more knowledge about visual appearance than about any other single topic. One of the greatest challenges of computer vision research may be to develop ways to accumulate and make efficient use of this vast quantity of knowledge.

BIBLIOGRAPHIC INDEX

Each of the following references is followed by a list of the page numbers on which it is cited.

[Attneave, 1954] Attneave, Fred, "Some informational aspects of visual perception," *Psychological Review,* **61** (1954), 183-193. *(cited pp. 25, 57)*

[Barlow & Reeves, 1979]
Barlow, H.B., and B.C. Reeves, "The versatility and absolute efficiency of detecting mirror symmetry in random dot displays," *Vision Research,* **19** (1979), 783-793. *(cited p. 30)*

[Barnard, 1983] Barnard, Stephen T., "Interpreting perspective images," *Artificial Intelligence,* **21** (1983), 435-462. *(cited p. 80)*

[Barrow & Tenenbaum, 1981]
Barrow, H.G. and J.M. Tenenbaum, "Interpreting line drawings as three-dimensional surfaces," *Artificial Intelligence,* **17** (1981), 75-116. *(cited p. 75)*

[Biederman, 1981]
Biederman, Irving, "On the semantics of a glance at a scene," in *Perceptual Organization,* Kubovy & Pomerantz, Eds. (Hillsdale, N.J.: Lawrence Erlbaum, 1981), 213-253. *(cited p. 109)*

[Binford, 1971] Binford, Thomas O., "Visual perception by computer," Invited paper at *IEEE Systems Science and Cybernetics Conference*, Miami, December 1971. *(cited p. 99)*

[Binford, 1981] Binford, Thomas O., "Inferring surfaces from images," *Artificial Intelligence*, **17** (1981), 205-244. *(cited p. 75, 85)*

[Brady, 1983] Brady, M., "Criteria for representations of shape," in *Human and Machine Vision*, Beck, Hope & Rosenfeld, Eds. (New York: Academic Press, 1983), 39-84. *(cited p. 30)*

[Brooks, 1981] Brooks, Rodney A., "Symbolic reasoning among 3-D models and 2-D images," *Artificial Intelligence*, **17** (1981), 285-348. *(cited pp. 19, 96, 116, 127, 134)*

[Brooks, 1982] Brooks, Rodney A., "Representing possible realities for vision and manipulation," *IEEE Pattern Recognition and Image Processing Conference*, (Las Vegas, June 1982), 587–592. *(cited p. 98)*

[Bruce & Morgan, 1975]
Bruce, Vicky G. and Michael J. Morgan, "Violations of symmetry and repetition in visual patterns," *Perception*, **4** (1975), 239-249. *(cited p. 30)*

[Bundesen & Larsen, 1975]
Bundesen, Claus and Axel Larsen, "Visual transformation of size," *Journal of Experimental Psychology: Human Perception and Performance*, **1** (1975), 214–220. *(cited p. 114)*

[Charniak, 1983]
Charniak, Eugene, "The Bayesian basis of common sense medical diagnosis," *Proceedings of AAAI-83* (Washington, D.C., August, 1983), 70-73. *(cited p. 103)*

[Clark & Hummel, 1984]
Clark, Dayton and Robert Hummel, "VSH user's manual: an image processing environment," *Robotics Research Technical Report*, Courant Institute, New York University (September 1984). *(cited p. 135)*

[Clowes, 1971]   Clowes, M.B. "On seeing things," *Artificial Intelligence,* **2** (1971), 79-116. *(cited p. 74)*

[Cooper & Shepard, 1984]
                    Cooper, Lynn A., and Roger N. Shepard, "Turning something over in the mind," *Scientific American,* **251,** 6 (December 1984), 106–114. *(cited p. 112)*

[Draper, 1981]   Draper, Stephen W., "The use of gradient and dual space in line-drawing interpretation," *Artificial Intelligence,* **17** (1981), 461-508. *(cited p. 74)*

[Duda & Hart, 1972]
                    Duda, R.O. and P.E. Hart, "Use of the Hough transformation to detect lines and curves in pictures," *Communications of ACM,* **15,** 1 (1972), 11-15. *(cited p. 29)*

[Fischler & Bolles, 1981]
                    Fischler, Martin A. and Robert C. Bolles, "Random sample consensus: A paradigm for model fitting with applications to image analysis and automated cartography," *Communications of the ACM,* **24,** 6 (1981), 381-395. *(cited pp. 117, 129)*

[Funt, 1983]   Funt, Brian, "A parallel-process model of mental rotation," *Cognitive Science,* **7** (1983), 67–93. *(cited p. 114)*

[Ganapathy, 1984]
                    Ganapathy, Sundaram, "Decomposition of transformation matrices for robot vision," *Proc. of IEEE Conference on Robotics* (Atlanta, 1984), 130-139. *(cited p. 117)*

[Goad, 1983]   Goad, Chris, "Special purpose automatic programming for 3D model-based vision," *Proceedings ARPA Image Understanding Workshop* (1983). Revised version to appear in *From Pixels to Predicates,* Alex Pentland, Ed. (Ablex Publishing Co., 1985). *(cited pp. 19, 95, 129, 134)*

[Gottlieb *et al.,* 1983]
                    Gottlieb, Allan, *et al.,* "The NYU Ultracomputer— designing an MIMD shared memory parllel computer," *IEEE Transactions on Computers,* **C-32**,2 (1983), 175–189. *(cited p. 147)*

[Grimson & Lozano-Pérez, 1983]
Grimson, Eric, and Thomás Lozano-Pérez, "Model-based recognition and localization from sparse range or tactile data," *MIT AI Memo 738* (August 1983). *(cited p. 97)*

[Hochberg, 1957]
Hochberg, Julian E., "Effects of the Gestalt revolution: The Cornell symposium on perception," *Psychological Review*, **64**, 2 (1957), 73-84. *(cited p. 25)*

[Hochberg & Brooks, 1962]
Hochberg, Julian E. and Virginia Brooks, "Pictorial recognition as an unlearned ability: A study of one child's performance," *American Journal of Psychology*, **75** (1962), 624-628. *(cited p. 15)*

[Hoffman, 1983] Hoffman, Donald D., *Representing Shapes for Visual Recognition*, Ph.D. Thesis, Massachusetts Institute of Technology (May 1983). *(cited p. 57)*

[Huffman, 1971] Huffman, D.A., "Impossible objects as nonsense sentences," *Machine Intelligence*, **6** (1971), 295-323. *(cited p. 74)*

[Julesz, 1981] Julesz, Bela, "Figure and ground perception in briefly presented isodipole textures," in *Perceptual Organization*, Kubovy & Pomerantz, Eds. (Hillsdale, N.J.: Lawrence Erlbaum, 1981), 27-54. *(cited p. 45)*

[Kanade, 1981] Kanade, Takeo, "Recovery of the three-dimensional shape of an object from a single view," *Artificial Intelligence*, **17** (1981), 409-460. *(cited pp. 74, 84)*

[Kanizsa, 1979] Kanizsa, Gaetano, *Organization in Vision* (New York: Praeger, 1979). *(cited p. 23)*

[Katz, 1950] Katz, David, *Gestalt Psychology: Its Nature and Significance* (New York: Ronald Press Co., 1950). *(cited p. 24)*

[Leeper, 1935] Leeper, Robert, "A study of a neglected portion of the field of learning—the development of sensory organization," *Journal of Genetic Psychology*, **46** (1935), 41-75. *(cited p. 18)*

[Leeuwenberg & Buffart, 1983]
Leeuwenberg, Emanuel and Hans Buffart, "The perception of foreground and background as derived from structural information theory," *Internal Report,* Department of Experimental Psychology, University of Nijmegen, The Netherlands (1983). *(cited p. 25)*

[Lowe, 1980]   Lowe, David G., "Solving for the parameters of object models from image descriptions," *Proc. ARPA Image Understanding Workshop* (College Park, MD, April 1980), 121–127. *(for reference)*

[Lowe & Binford, 1981]
Lowe, David G. and Thomas O. Binford, "The interpretation of three-dimensional structure from image curves," *Proceedings of IJCAI-7* (Vancouver: August 1981), 613-618. *(cited p. 27)*

[Lowe & Binford, 1982]
Lowe, David G. and Thomas O. Binford, "Segmentation and aggregation: An approach to figure-ground phenomena," *Proc. ARPA Image Understanding Workshop,* (Stanford, Calif., Sept. 1982). *(cited p. 46)*

[Lowe & Binford, 1983]
Lowe, David G. and Thomas O. Binford, "Perceptual organization as a basis for visual recognition," *Proceedings of AAAI-83* (Washington, D.C., August 1983), 255–260. *(for reference)*

[Lowrance & Garvey, 1982]
Lowrance, John D. and Thomas D. Garvey, "Evidential reasoning: A developing concept," *IEEE Proceedings of the International Converence on Cybernetics and Society* (October 1982), 6-9. *(cited p. 103)*

[Mackworth, 1973]
Mackworth, A.K., "Interpreting pictures of polyhedral scenes," *Artificial Intelligence,* 4 (1973), 121-137. *(cited p. 74)*

[Marimont, 1982]
Marimont, David H., "Segmentation in ACRONYM," *Proc. ARPA Image Understanding Workshop* (Stanford, Calif., September 1982). *(cited pp. 55, 70)*

[Marimont, 1984]
Marimont, David, "A representation for image curves," *Proc. AAAI-84* (Austin, Texas: August, 1984). *(cited pp. 59, 71)*

[Marr, 1976]
Marr, David, "Early processing of visual information," *Philosophical Transactions of the Royal Society of London, Series B,* **275** (1976), 483-524. *(cited pp. 28, 45, 47)*

[Marr, 1977]
Marr, David, "Artificial intelligence—A personal view," *Artificial Intelligence,* **9** (1977), 37-48. *(cited p. 7)*

[Marr & Hildreth, 1980]
Marr, David, and Ellen Hildreth, "Theory of edge detection," *Proc. Royal Society of London, B,* **207** (1980), 187-217. *(cited pp. 135, 142)*

[Marr, 1982]
Marr, David, *Vision* (San Francisco: W.H. Freeman and Co., 1982). *(cited pp. 7, 10, 14, 29, 46, 47)*

[Morgan, 1983]
Morgan, Michael J., "Mental rotation: A computationally plausible account of transformation through intermediate steps," *Perception,* **12** (1983), 203-211. *(cited p. 114)*

[Palmer, 1983]
Palmer, Stephen E., "The psychology of perceptual organization: A transformational approach," in *Human and Machine Vision,* Beck, Hope & Rosenfeld, Eds., (New York: Academic Press, 1983), 269-339. *(cited p. 28)*

[Pavlidis, 1977]
Pavlidis, T., *Structural Pattern Recognition* (New York: Springer-Verlag, 1977). *(cited p. 54)*

[Roberts, 1966]
Roberts, L.G., "Machine perception of three-dimensional objects," in *Optical and Electro-optical Information Processing,* Tippet *et al.,* Eds. (Cambridge, Mass.: MIT Press, 1966), 159-197. *(cited pp. 19, 134)*

[Rutkowski & Rosenfeld, 1978]
Rutkowski, W.S., and Azriel Rosenfeld, "A comparison of corner-detection techniques for chain-coded curves," *TR-623,* Computer Science Center, University of Maryland, 1978. *(cited pp. 54, 63)*

[Salamin, 1979] Salamin, Gene, "Application of quaternions to computation with rotations," *Internal working paper, Stanford Artificial Intelligence Laboratory*, 1979. *(cited p. 119)*

[Shafer, 1976] Shafer, Glenn, *A Mathematical Theory of Evidence*, (Princeton, N.J.: Princeton University Press, 1976). *(cited p. 103)*

[Shafer, 1982] Shafer, Steven A. and Takeo Kanade, "Using shadows in finding surface orientations," CMU-CS-82-100, Computer Science Dept., Carnegie-Mellon University (January 1982). *(cited p. 89)*

[Shepard & Metzler, 1971]
Shepard R. N. and J. Metzler, "Mental rotation of three-dimensional objects," *Science*, **171** (1971), 701-703. *(cited p. 112)*

[Shirai, 1978] Shirai, Y., "Recognition of man-made objects using edge cues," in *Computer Vision Systems*, A. Hanson, E. Riseman, eds. (New York: Academic Press, 1978). *(cited pp. 19, 54, 63, 135)*

[Shortliffe & Buchanan, 1975]
Shortliffe, Edward H. and Bruce G. Buchanan, "A model of inexact reasoning in medicine," *Mathematical Biosciences*, **23** (1975), 355-356. *(cited p. 103)*

[Stevens, 1978] Stevens, Kent A., "Computation of locally parallel structure," *Biological Cybernetics*, **29** (1978), 19-28. *(cited p. 46)*

[Stevens, 1981] Stevens, Kent A., "The visual interpretation of surface contours," *Artificial Intelligence*, **17** (1981), 47-73. *(cited p. 27)*

[Sugihara, 1978] Sugihara, K., "Quantitative analysis of line drawings of polyhedral scenes," *Proc. Fourth Int. Joint Conference on Pattern Recognition*, (Kyoto, 1978), 771-773. *(cited p. 74)*

[Szolovitz & Pauker, 1978]
Szolovitz, Peter and S. G. Pauker, "Categorical and probabilistic reasoning in medical diagnosis," *Artificial Intelligence*, **11** (1978), 115-144. *(cited p. 103)*

[Treisman, 1982]

Treisman, Anne, "Perceptual grouping and attention in visual search for features and objects," *Journal of Experimental Psychology: Human Perception and Performance*, **8**, 2 (1982), 194–214. *(cited p. 45)*

[Ullman, 1979] Ullman, S., *The Interpretation of Visual Motion* (Cambridge, Mass.: MIT Press, 1979). *(cited p. 27)*

[Walter & Tropf, 1983]

Walter, I. and H. Tropf, "3-D recognition of randomly oriented parts," *Proceedings of the Third International Conf. on Robot Vision and Sensory Controls* (November, 1983, Cambridge, Mass.), 193–200. *(cited p. 135)*

[Waltz, 1975] Waltz, D., "Understanding line drawings of scenes with shadows," *The Psychology of Computer Vision*, Ed. P.H. Winston (McGraw-Hill, 1975). *(cited p. 74)*

[Wertheimer, 1923]

Wertheimer, Max, "Untersuchungen zur Lehe von der Gestalt II," *Psychol. Forsch.*, **4** (1923). Translated as "Principles of perceptual organization" in *Readings in Perception*, David Beardslee and Michael Wertheimer, Eds., (Princeton, N.J.: 1958), 115-135. *(cited p. 22)*

[Witkin, 1982] Witkin, Andrew P., "Intensity-based edge classification," *Proceedings of AAAI-82*, Pittsburgh, August 1982, 36-41. *(cited p. 76)*

[Witkin, 1983] Witkin, Andrew P., "Scale-space filtering," *Proc. IJCAI-83* (Karlsruhe, West Germany: August, 1983), 1019-22. *(cited pp. 54, 72)*

[Witkin & Tenenbaum, 1983]

Witkin, Andrew P. and Jay M. Tenenbaum, "On the role of structure in vision," in *Human and Machine Vision*, Beck, Hope & Rosenfeld, Eds. (New York: Academic Press, 1983), 481-543. Abridged version appears as "What is perceptual organization for?" *IJCAI-83* (Karlsruhe, West Germany: August, 1983), 1023-26. *(cited pp. 26, 33, 39)*

[Wolf, 1983] Wolf, Paul R., *Elements of Photogrammetry* (New York: McGraw-Hill, 1983). *(cited p. 116)*

[Zucker, 1983]   Zucker, Steven W., "Computational and psychophys-
                    ical experiments in grouping: Early orientation selec-
                    tion," in *Human and Machine Vision*, Beck, Hope &
                    Rosenfeld, Eds. (New York: Academic Press, 1983),
                    545-567. *(cited p. 29)*